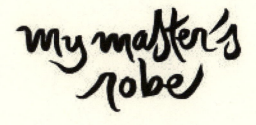

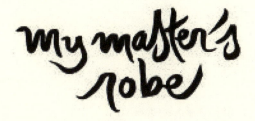

My Master's Robe

Memories of a Novice Monk

by

THICH NHAT HANH

Foreword by SISTER ANNABEL LAITY

Parallax Press
Berkeley, California

Parallax Press
P.O. Box 7355
Berkeley, California 94707
www.parallax.org

Parallax Press is the publishing division of Unified Buddhist Church, Inc.

Cover design and illustrations by Nguyen Thi Hop and Nguyen Dong.
Text design by Nguyen Dong.

Special thanks to the sisters at Green Mountain Dharma Center
and the volunteers of La Boi Press for translating the stories
from the Vietnamese language.

Library of Congress Cataloging-in-Publication Data
Nhât Hanh, Thích.
    [Tinh Nguoi: English]
    My Master's Robe / by Thich Nhat Hanh.
        p. cm.
    Translation of Tinh Nguoi.
    ISBN 1-888375-03-5 (pbk.)
        1. Nhât Hanh, Thích. 2. Buddhist novices—Vietnam—Biography.
    3. Monastic and religious life (Buddhism)—Vietnam. 4. Priests,
    Buddhist—Vietnam—Biography. I. Title.

BQ962.H36 A3 2002
294.3'657'092—dc21

           2002002678

1 2 3 4 5 6 7 8 9 10 / 06 05 04 03 02

CONTENTS

FOREWORD

Written by the author in his late twenties, these stories first appeared in *Phat Giao Buddhist Magazine* between 1956 and 1959. The stories were collected in a book titled *Tinh Nguoi* (Vietnamese) and published in 1964 by La Boi Press, Saigon. Tinh nguoi means "humanity" and the stories are about just that — humanity in the midst of war and violence.

This subject is pertinent to us in our own time. In the face of terrorism, what lessons can we learn from the different spiritual paths of the world? Terrorism could break out anywhere at anytime; it is always available even if dormant. When given the right causes and conditions, the seeds of terrorism sprout and we have to deal with a living hell. Whether perpetrated unofficially by a relatively small group of individuals or by a large army sanctioned by the state, terrorism can only be responded to by human love. Human love is also always available, and we can recognize that we are one humanity — that all mothers everywhere suffer when their sons are killed in war.

My Master's Robe is set in the heart of a peaceful monastery that is surrounded by war during the years from 1942–1947. The French fought a bitter war to maintain their sovereignty in Vietnam from 1946–1954. The people of Vietnam were terrorized by the colonialists, and no doubt the French soldiers suffered bitterly at the hands of the Viet Minh. It was at a time when in France the aftermath of the Second World War was still lingering heavily. This is what is meant by the sentence spoken by the young French soldier in Chapter Ten: "Seeing the people here work so hard to rebuild their shattered lives reminds me of the shattered lives of my relatives in France."

The author describes his encounter with this young French soldier in 1947. He himself was still young, a fully-ordained Buddhist monk of twenty-one years-old or so. The author says outright in this chapter that at the time he did not like French soldiers very much. French soldiers had raided the monasteries for food and had executed monks belonging to the resistance movement, sometimes in very cruel ways. The monks of the author's monastery had been forced to evacuate for several months. In spite of this, he embraced the young French soldier he met as a true friend and a brother.

In 1946–47, young monks and nuns wanted to save their country from foreign domination. Institutes of Buddhist Studies were closed so that the student monks and nuns could devote more time to demonstrations and meetings supporting the national movement for independence. At the same time, the Buddhist monastery provided a nectar of compassion for the Vietnamese people during these years. The peaceful life of the monastery, where true brotherhood was possible, was a small oasis in the midst of the suffering of war. To say that it was a small oasis refers only to the space that the monastery occupied. In terms of the far-reaching effect of the monastic practice at that time and the implications it would have in the future, the oasis could be conceived of as very great.

Fifty-five years after the events recounted in this book, the author continues to live and shape the monastic life to reflect the good in the world. He has not shirked his responsibility for one moment. After the terrorist attacks in New York on September 11, 2001, he called for a ten-day fast and led ceremonies for those who died or were injured. He visited New York to help people deal with their fear and anger and to support those who cared for the victims of the tragedy and the bereaved. His message was basically the same as we find in the conversations he had in the 1940s with his monk brother, Tam Man, and the young French soldier in this book.

In some of the conversations between the author and Brother Tam Man there are references to the Ly and Tran eras. The Ly and Tran eras lasted from the tenth to the end of the fourteenth century in Dai Viet, the country that was the precursor of modern Vietnam. The Tran kings, and the Ly kings before them, were

Buddhists. Under their rule, the country of Dai Viet, just freed from Chinese rule, enjoyed a period of peace, prosperity, and independence.[1] These eras were an inspiration to the author of this book and his contemporaries in the movement seeking independence from colonial rule in the twentieth century, and they are an inspiration to practicing Buddhists in our own time.

In *My Master's Robe* there are some references to the physical hardships endured by the monks practicing in Hue in the 1940s, but these physical hardships never for a moment induced the author to consider giving up his aspiration to live his life as a monk. When recently visiting Vietnam, I heard an elderly nun recount how the author, dressed in thin, inadequate clothing, had come back from herding the cows one day. He was shivering so much that his knees knocked together. Despite these small hardships, the beauty and joy of the monastic life never left him. This book is a testimony to the spiritual love and brotherhood found within the monastery as well as to the deep joy and happiness that comes from involvement in the daily monastic practice.

Outside the monastery the real hardship was the suffering of war and, like it or not, the young monk could never forget that. In his poem, "The Fruit of Awareness Is Ripe,"[2] he likens his

[1] For more on fourteenth century Vietnam, see Thich Nhat Hanh, *Hermitage Among the Clouds: An Historical Novel of Fourteenth Century Vietnam* (Berkeley, CA: Parallax Press, 1993).
[2] See Thich Nhat Hanh, *Call Me by My True Names* (Berkeley, CA: Parallax Press, 1999).

youthful years to an unripe, green plum that the suffering of war bit into, leaving its tooth marks behind. The poem continues:

> *But since I have learned how to love,*
> *The door of my soul has been left wide open*
> *to the winds of the four directions.*
> *The situation is calling out for revolution.*
> *The fruit of awareness is already ripe,*
> *and the door can never be closed again.*

The "winds of the four directions" could refer to the suffering brought about by the three poisons of craving, hatred, and ignorance, which result in war and violence. "The situation calls for revolution" could be an allusion to the colonial status of Vietnam and perhaps to Buddhism, too. The author has said that a monk is a revolutionary, but not in a political sense. The revolution is not political but spiritual. It is to change our ways of thinking and consuming. Buddhism needed to renew itself sixty years ago in order to meet the needs of the fast-changing world then, and it still needs to renew itself in our own time. "The door can never be closed," means that once understanding of the situation of our world has given rise to compassion we have no alternative but to act to relieve the suffering.

A young monk or nun learns in the monastery how to love. His or her teachers and brothers and sisters in the practice are there to help him or her learn this. The monastery can be the ideal place to provide such training. In this little book we see how the pure love of a teacher can fill the young monk's heart with a deep aspiration to devote his life to serving those who suffer in the world. The books on monastic discipline, when studied and practiced, provide monks and nuns with the means to put their aspiration into practice. Eventually the love is no longer contained within the monastery but also flows out into the world.

We can all train ourselves in love by learning the way to listen deeply in order to understand the situation and the suffering of the one we consider to be our enemy, and we can train ourselves to speak lovingly. The place of the monastery is to help us do this — it is a workshop that creates the practices that the world needs. A monk who was a peace activist in Vietnam trained a cat and a mouse to live together peacefully in a cage. He asked, Why then can't human beings be trained to live peacefully on this planet Earth?

I wish that this little book can be your inspiration, as it has been mine, leading you through delightful and often amusing stories to see your own place in the task of relieving the suffering in this world.

Sister Annabel Laity, Abbess
Green Mountain Dharma Center
June 2002

CATTLE TENDING

Our temple used to have four cows. The cow barn was near the pineapple garden and sometimes on a blazing hot afternoon Brother Tam Man would invite me to go down to the pineapple garden to sit under the shade of the trees. There the two of us would skin a pineapple and eat it, watching the mother cow as she pondered life while her calves lingered near the barn. The truth was, the temple didn't raise cows for their milk or for their meat — we were all vegetarians, apart from the black cat. The cat wasn't ours; we didn't know when or how he came, but he was determined to stay. As for the cows, we kept them for their manure for the garden, that was all. The soil of the Spring of Yang Hill, where the temple was located, was full of stones and pebbles, and without compost nothing could grow well. With the manure we made compost to grow cassava and potatoes.

Those who joined the community had to pass a period of taking care of the cows for at least three months. Even if you were weak and thin, you had to agree to this term. Each day, while everyone else went about their tasks of sweeping, dusting, or gardening, the person in charge of the cattle would open the stable door and herd the cow and her calves to the grassy side of the mountain. Three months after I came to the temple, I got to take care of the cows. Saying that "I got to" do it isn't an exaggeration. Relatively speaking, watching the cows was easy work and it offered me plenty of time to study.

Each morning, balancing a pole on my shoulders with a large bag on either end and a sickle in my hand, I took the cows into the hills. The book on monastic discipline called *The Essential Vinaya for Daily Use* was tucked inside one of the bags. When we reached a spot where there was plenty of grass, I'd let the cows graze freely. I put the book under a pine tree with a stone to weigh it down so the wind wouldn't blow it away, and then I'd take a bag and sickle and begin to cut fresh new sprouting leaves and twigs from all the bushes and trees and pack them tightly into the bag.

These leaves and twigs were used in place of straw because we couldn't find straw in the mountains. They were spread on the barn floor twice a day for the cows to lie on. When the leaves and twigs mixed with the cow manure, it made excellent compost for the garden. About every ten days four or five of us would collect this compost from the barn to store it in a composting house to decompose. Because our robes would have been too cumbersome for the job, we wore only shorts to do the work, and after we finished we went to the well for a good wash.

When the two bags were stuffed full to the brim with twigs and leaves, I would stop to rest under a shade tree. Usually I'd have to move to different places before there'd be enough new growth to fill the two large bags, so the work wasn't finished before 10:30. Then I'd rest and take out my book to study.

The *Vinaya* book was written in classical Chinese. This volume on monastic discipline, like other Buddhist texts, had to be memorized by heart. If you wanted to take the novice vows, you had to learn the early morning and afternoon liturgies by heart plus the four volumes contained in the *Lesser Vinaya: Essential Vinaya for Daily Use, Essentials of Novice Vinaya, Encouraging Words of Master Quy Son,* and *Fine Manners*. Only after you had flawlessly memorized these four books by heart and were able to respond to the teacher's questions on their content would you have any hope of taking the novice vows. If you could not do this, then no matter how old you were or how talented you were, you would be considered a *dieu*. A dieu is a practicing aspirant who is not yet accepted in the monastic circle.

When it rained it was very difficult to take care of the cows and collect twigs and leaves. Sometimes the weather was biting cold. I would put on a woolly sweater and a rain cape of palm leaves before I set out for the mountains. The book had to be kept deep inside the bag or it would be soaked by the rain and fall apart. To learn these four manuals by heart was really difficult and if you were lazy it was almost impossible. There were novices who, when they learned something new, forgot what they had learned before. I knew of a novice who took a year to learn the *Surangama Dharani* mantra yet still couldn't remember it. But then this mantra was truly difficult; not only was it in Sanskrit — that was bad enough — it was also six to seven times longer than the Great Compassion mantra. No wonder there was the proverb that said: Soldiers fear the frontier post, monks fear the Surangama Dharani! The truth was that I didn't fear the Surangama Dharani, and although I was busy, I managed to learn it by heart within a fortnight. Brother Man was awestruck. He didn't have a methodic way of memorizing, so it took him longer than a month to learn it.

One day when I was tending the cows, there was a sudden downpour that startled the mother cow and she suddenly ran off, the calves chasing behind her. Afraid of losing them, I chased after them. Who knows what made her run this way? She had no intention of returning; she just kept on running. The young calves in the meantime ran off in different directions. I had only been on the job for a month and I did not understand the strange habits of cows. How was I was to deal with this? I ran so hard that my legs ached and I was completely exhausted, but if I gave up, I was afraid I would lose the cow; still, if I chased after her, how was I to know where she would take me? In the end, I had to hire two farmers to help capture the cow and lure her back. Luckily when I returned to Nam Giao Hill I found the young calves still roaming there, and they followed us home. That evening I locked them all in the barn and did not allow them to graze on grass.

It was during this time while I was tending the cows that I memorized by heart the four volumes of the *Lesser Vinaya*. I was able to learn the last volume, *Encouraging Words of Master Quy Son,* very fast because the literature was so beautiful and it was written in lyrics that were easy to memorize. During that period, I would have a late lunch with Brother Man after returning from the mountains with the cows and then we would recite the lines together.

Each day the temple bell and a small drum resonated out into the mountains to mark the time when the rice offering was being made to the Buddha by one of the monks. At that moment I was usually studying the manual of mindful verses. I'd put the book down and listen to the clear sound of the bell being carried by the wind and the warm low sound of the drum. Then came three sounds of a wooden board that echoed and shook the forest and mountains. The three sounds from the board signaled it was time for lunch and for me to return to the temple. Placing the pole with the bags of twigs and leaves on my shoulders, I would round up the cows and slowly return home.

At the barn I would spread the twigs and leaves on the floor and close the fence. Then I'd have a wash at the well and go up to the dining room. By that time the rest of the community had finished eating and were resting in their rooms. Brother Man, who was our teacher's attendant, ate his lunch after the others, the same as I did. We ate at a table in the back of the dining room, as the front was where the higher monks sat. The meal consisted of pressed rice with two different dishes: boiled green leaves that we dipped in a salty sauce, a stir fry, salty stew, or soup. The pressed rice was formed from two bowls of packed rice that were compressed tightly together. It was equivalent to four average small bowls of rice.

Most times we would relish the food. I ate until I was full, partly from hunger, and partly because of the bright and smiling eyes of Brother Tam Man.

Some days when the afternoons were cool, Brother Tam Man would come to the mountains to spend time with me after work meditation. These were truly some of the most joyful moments of my life. Joyful, perhaps, because doing so was not quite in accordance with the rules. He would bring a few baked potatoes that had fragrant brown skins and were very delicious. The two of us would sit on a hill, keeping an eye on the cows and enjoying the potatoes. We'd get very thirsty after eating, but because the water on the mountain wasn't drinkable, we would herd the cows back earlier than usual and go to the kitchen for some tea. Auntie Tu would ask, "What have you young brothers been doing to make you so thirsty?"

Tending the cattle was a relatively easy task compared to some of my other jobs at the temple. When I first came, I had to draw well water and carry it to the kitchen, which was about four or five hundred yards away. I started off with buckets that were only half-full, suspended on each end of a carrying pole that rested on my shoulders. After three days I worked up to carrying full buckets. My apprentice shoulders were red and swollen. It was so painful that it was better to shoulder two full buckets of water than two empty ones! It took many weeks for my shoulders to heal.

Another difficult task was polishing rice. This was a manual process that required a team effort of four or five people, each pounding grains of rice in a large mortar with big pestles to whiten the grain. As far as Brother Man and I were concerned, these pestles were too heavy. Yet it had to be lifted and pounded in rhythm and at the right time. When the pestle wasn't well aimed, the rice would jump everywhere. Either that or the pestle came down at an angle, and if it wasn't lifted up right away, it might collide with the pestle of the person next to you, who was about to pound his down. After fifty or sixty hits with the pestle, our entire bodies would be exhausted and we'd be soaked in sweat. It was clearly the worst job.

Then there were other kinds of work that everyone had to do. For example, there was hulling rice and digging earth to grow the different types of potatoes. My temple followed the Zen tradition; therefore every one of us from the highest monk to the newest member equally followed the principle of "no work, no food."

We all knew the story of the ancestral teacher Pai Chang. He worked with the community in the garden, growing vegetables and cutting peas every day even though he was eighty years old. Seeing him working so hard, the monks became concerned. But they knew if they asked him to rest, he wouldn't listen. So one day the monks hid all his tools. Without his tools he could no longer work in the garden. But that day he didn't eat his meal. Nor did he eat the next day or the day after that.

The monks thought, "Maybe the Venerable Teacher is vexed because we have hidden all his tools." So they returned the tools and the Venerable Teacher went out to work the very next day, and that afternoon he ate lunch. In the evening he gave a teaching to the community on "no work, no food."

The community's livelihood depended on gardening and the rice field. The rice field was far from the temple so we had to hire people to take care of it. In return for their work, the temple would share the harvest with them. We cared for the garden ourselves. We grew many different kinds of food, including tea, jackfruit, sweet potatoes, and cassava.

We all worked, but we didn't work all day. There was time for us to study the sutras, practice writing, listen to the teachings given by our teacher, chant, and meditate. Most important was meditation. My teacher taught that meditation was the door to understanding, and the career of monks and nuns.

Of course you did not practice sitting meditation all day when you entered the temple. For months and sometimes years you had to take care of the cows, collect dry twigs and leaves, carry water, pound rice, and collect wood for the fire. Every time my mother came to visit from our village, which was far away, she would regard these things as being the challenges of the first stage of practice. At first my mother was concerned for my health, but as I grew healthier, she stopped worrying about me. As for me, I knew that these were not challenges — they were themselves the practice. If you enter this life you will see for yourself. If there was no taking care of the cows, no collecting of twigs and leaves, no carrying water, no growing potatoes, then there would no means for the practice of meditation.

Brother Man saw it in the same way as I did, and later in life the two of us would look back on our novice years with deep affection, joy, and gratitude. .

BROTHER DUONG

After my duty of tending the cows ended, I returned the cattle to Brother Duong. Every dieu had to pass through a period of looking after the cows, and when it was over, the responsibility was handed back to Brother Duong. Although Brother Duong was close to forty years old, and even though he had come to the temple as a child, he was still only a *chu* — a young brother.

He was a very special person at the temple. All the novices were close to him. He laughed a lot and was very likable. He inspired me to think deeply about diligent practice and the effect of my daily actions in each moment. He had lost the use of his left hand, so he learned to do everything with his right hand. He could drop the water bucket down the well and pull

it up full of water, he could plow, and he could chop wood
— all with just one hand, using his left hand as a steadying
point.

When Brother Duong was not looking after the cows, he
did other work at the temple. He was happy with whatever
work the monks asked of him. Often Auntie Tu would ask
him to help supply water to the kitchen or find wood for the
fire. He was seldom around for the Dharma discussions and
personal conversations that took place within the community.
His sleeping quarters were in the bell tower on the same landing as the bell. Each morning it was his job to invite the Great
Bell and recite the *gathas*. His chanting voice was deep and
warm, perhaps the most wholehearted voice in the temple.

The Great Bell begins to sound.
Chanting the gatha the sound rises high,
Above it penetrates the realms of the gods,
Below it puts an end to the realms of great suffering.

In the early hours of the morning his chanting sent warmth
throughout the temple. I would get up at the first sound of
the bell, and though it was freezing cold, I would make my
way to the small kitchen near the dormitory to light a fire to
boil water and prepare tea for my teacher. Only after the fire

was blazing hot could I stop shaking. Then I would warm my hands over the fire and listen to the long sounds of the bell mingling with Brother Duong's voice.

As the sound of the bell is heard
The afflictions grow light
Understanding grows great
Awakening is born.

Boong... how strong and sustaining the early morning bell was, just like Brother Duong's chanting. There was not one person who after having heard these sounds would not rise immediately to prepare for sitting meditation or for chanting. Of course, sometimes we would oversleep because we had not heard the bell. Brother Duong would often say, "It's OK if you didn't hear the bell and overslept, but if you heard the bell and still went back to sleep, that's an offense." This offense, he told us, would result in our being reborn as a snake in the next lifetime, and we would have to lie flat on the ground forever and never be able to stand up. Then he would recite this verse:

If, having heard the bell, you continue to lie in bed,
The Dharma protectors and good spirits will be displeased.

Your merit in this life being weakened,
You will have the body of a snake in the next life.

Hearing this verse was enough to make a shiver run up your spine, and no one dared to get back under the covers to sleep more!

Everyone at the temple got up at four in the morning. While Brother Duong invited the Great Bell, Brother Man and I took turns making tea and Brother Giai made the incense offering in the meditation hall. The high monks sat and meditated while the Great Bell sounded; when it stopped, the teachers came out of their rooms for tea and got ready for the morning practice session. Some people who were studying didn't attend this session, but Brother Duong never missed it. He followed the path of "merit" and refused to study anymore. He put all his effort into making merit, inviting the bell, and attending the chanting periods. When the last bell was sounded, he would enter the Buddha Hall through a side door to join the community in chanting. Standing at the front of the hall, with my palms joined together, I could hear his wholehearted chanting very clearly. At first he wasn't always able to follow the rhythm of the drum; but soon his efforts succeeded, and his voice blended with the voices of the rest of the community.

Later on when I was at the Buddhist Institute of Bao Quoc, I would return to visit the temple twice a month. I had become a brother by then, and you might say that I studied better and advanced faster than Brother Duong, yet I always continued to respect him as an older brother. I often shared my feelings with Brother Man about Brother Duong. "We study more, but our ability to maintain awareness is definitely not as good as Brother Duong's," I would tell him. "Who knows, one day we may meet him in another lifetime, and have to admit that although we traveled faster, we arrived later."

One day when I was watching Brother Duong build a fence for the cows, I said to him, "When you become a Buddha, remember to take me to the shore of liberation, Brother." It was a sincere statement but he thought that I was joking. He smiled as if he liked the joke. It upset me. "Honestly, Brother Duong, I mean it!" But still he wouldn't believe me. So I had to accept that.

I remembered the story of how the Sixth Patriarch Hui Neng had practiced long ago. He wasn't a scholar, nor did he have any schooling, but as a result of his determined practice of carrying water, chopping wood, and pounding rice, his wisdom radiated naturally, and the *sanghati* robe and begging bowl were passed to him from Patriarch Hung-jen to represent his enlightenment. I had the feeling that, no matter where

I was many lifetimes from now, if I returned to my temple I would still find Brother Duong with the same way of being, the same smile, and the same firm faith. Brother Duong was like a long-living tree with a powerful energy that fascinated me.

We never talked with Brother Duong about Dharma philosophy. I felt that he didn't need to hear or know it, though he often told us, "I am very happy for you, Brothers; you have the opportunity to study the sublime Dharma. Me, I am always the same." He didn't know that we never felt proud of our "sublime" study. We just wondered if we would ever be as solid as he was on our difficult path of practice. Just looking at him, we knew that his life would always be as solid as it was at that very moment.

Brother Duong attended to all his work with great care. The evening bell had to be invited for exactly 108 sounds. Brother Duong, I knew, was very careful about this. Under the bell stand he hung a steel wire with 108 tags on it. Each time one sound of the bell was invited he would slide a tag from the left to the right side, until he had invited the bell 108 times, and then he would recite the verse for ending the bell sounding. There were even more bells in the morning. Brother Duong said, "The sounds of the morning bells have to follow fast upon each other in order to hasten all the spirits back to their abode before the sun rises." For me, the virtue of these sounds following fast on each other in the morning was to give us energy and drive away laziness.

There were mornings when I would go out with Brother Duong to the mountains to gather wood. Using a very long hook, he would haul down the dry pine branches from very high in the trees. The branches made sharp cracking noises as they broke and fell, and sometimes we had to run to avoid being hit. I would gather all the branches together and the two of us would each shoulder a large load of wood and carry it back to the temple.

While I was writing this, Brother Duong was still living at the temple, as healthy as a long-living tree, though he had grown a lot older. Brother Duong belonged to a generation that did not have to concern itself with current affairs. He didn't have to see or hear the things that Brother Man and I had to see and hear. We had to think about complicated matters such as how to keep Buddhism alive and how to engage Buddhism with everyday life like it used to be during the Ly and Tran dynasties. We had to think about our studies, the practice, exams, the Dharma, and how to reorganize the Buddhist congregation. We had to concern ourselves with so much, and yet we didn't know whether anything could be accomplished. We had been invaded by society and the times.

The questioning of the collective consciousness of our time became the questioning of our individual consciousness. That is why I think I cherished even more the calm, quiet, and upright way of the life of Brother Duong. People in his generation involved themselves in resolving their individual problems as though they were the most important things in the world. Indeed, people have the right to do this.

As I write these lines, I know that my soul is not as peaceful as Brother Duong's. This is an advantage he has over me, and how I wish for it. Perhaps if he were to read this, he'd smile and think I was exaggerating. But the truth is, my generation was less fortunate than his. There is no way that we can close the window that has been opened for us. How can we ignore this life, the life that made young Siddhartha restless and eager to find a Way to liberate all beings?

THE LIZARD

Every day at precisely midday, Novice Tam Man, dressed in his gray robe, would ceremoniously bring a bowl of rice to the Ancestor's Hall and place it on the central altar. Then as a reminder to me, he would say, "It is time to offer rice to the Buddha, dear Brother." Having said this he would look at me and smile, then make his way to the dining hall to take care of the noon meal for the community. I would smile back and put down my writing brush, stack all my books and sutras into a neat pile, and prepare for the noon offering. My responsibility in the temple was to offer rice to the Buddha at midday. Novice Tam Man helped in the dining room: he set out the food, and when the rice offering was finished he would invite three sounds on the wooden board to indicate it was time for lunch.

Today when Novice Tam Man brought the bowl of rice

his expression was one of reflection and his usual smile was not there. I took the bowl from his hands, expressed my thanks, and watched him as he walked back to the building below. Our spirits were low because of what had occurred yesterday.

A fortnight ago, I was putting out the candles after having made the rice offering to the Buddha, when I saw a small lizard jump from the offering bowl with a few grains of rice in his mouth. He looked at me in panic, his eyes as bright as crystals. I did not shoo him away but he quickly ran behind the statue of the Buddha. I thought that this was an unusual occurrence, but the very next day when putting out the candles, I saw the lizard jump from the bowl of rice again. The same little mouth was stealing a couple of snowy-white rice grains. The same two eyes, as bright as tiny crystal balls, looked at me with panic.

The day after that I decided to keep watch. I placed the bowl of rice on the altar, but I did not take the lid off right away. I lit the candles and the incense and respectfully prostrated to the Buddha as usual. Then I invited three sounds of the bell and took the lid off the bowl. The little lizard was nowhere to be seen. I began to invite the bell and the wooden drum, and chanted the incense offering followed by the Mantra of Great Compassion. Then, appearing and disappearing behind the incense burner were the two tiny, bright crystal eyes

again. I calmly continued to chant the Mantra of Great Compassion, acting as though I had not seen a thing. Little mister lizard slowly began to edge his way up to the offering bowl. His tiny head teetered momentarily on the rim, and in an instant he jumped and fitted himself with ease into the bowl.

That day I performed the offering chant mindlessly. My mouth was chanting but my mind was on the lizard. I felt as if I was showing disrespect to the Three Jewels by my lack of concentration, but I couldn't help thinking that he was spoiling the rice offering to the Buddha. I was very angry at the naughty lizard for disturbing me this way. There were moments when I wanted to get up and chase him away, but I finished the Offering and Sharing the Merit chants as though a spiritual force held my knees to the floor.

The following day, I vowed not to open the lid of the bowl. After lighting the candles and the incense, I knelt down and invited the opening sounds of the bells and wooden drum and began to chant as usual. Then the same mister lizard from the previous days appeared from behind the incense burner and advanced towards the rice bowl. The tiny crystal-bright eyes looked in bewilderment at the cover on the bowl. He looked around for a moment and then mister lizard ran back behind the incense burner.

At first I felt elated because I had been able to get back

at the lizard for what he had done yesterday. But then I felt a pinch in my heart and I was full of regrets. There was something seemingly destructive, small-minded, and low that made my heart feel muddy. I felt painfully ill at ease and could not even look at the Buddha as I took the bowl of rice to leave.

I did not go to lunch; I said I was too tired.

Around one that afternoon, Tam Man came to see how I was doing. "Are you really so tired? I will make rice soup for you," he offered.

I beckoned Tam Man to sit by my bedside and asked, "Tam Man, every day we make a rice offering to the Buddha, but does the Buddha really receive our offering?"

"I'm certain of it, because if the Buddha doesn't receive it, then what is the use of making an offering everyday?" he replied. "Every temple has this ceremony of offering rice to the Buddha at midday."

"Then why is it that after the offering has been made, the rice remains untouched?" I asked. "Is it because the Buddha has not received it?"

"When we say 'to receive,' it doesn't mean 'to eat' it."

"Ah, that is so. But Brother Man...."

"Tell me what is on your mind," Brother Man interrupted, "I am listening."

"I did not think that the Buddha 'ate' the offering," I said, "but I didn't think he 'received' the offering either."

"I also thought that," Brother Man said. "Then one day when I took the bowl to fill it with rice for the offering, it suddenly occurred to me that when we make offerings to the Buddha it isn't the rice that we offer to the Buddha, but our sincerity of heart."

I took Tam Man's hand. "You are so right! Each day when we offer rice to the Buddha, it is as though the Buddha were still living and therefore we make the offering from our hearts. As the sutras say: 'The virtue of making offerings to the Buddhas is boundless.'"

"Then let me ask you this," Brother Tam Man said. "Why does it say in the sutras that 'To make offerings to all beings is to make offerings to the Buddha?' I don't really mean to challenge you," he added, "it is just something that I don't understand myself."

I became silent. My younger brother's question took me by surprise. It seemed like a simple question, yet one I couldn't easily answer. The vow of the Buddha was to relieve suffering and bring joy to all beings. To relieve the suffering in the world means to offer joy to the Buddhas. So why then had I kept the lid on the rice bowl and not allowed the lizard to take a few grains to feed himself?

Brother Tam Man was looking at me, waiting for a reply to his question. I smiled. "Well, what it means is that I should have opened the alms bowl and let the lizard share the rice, right?"

Brother Tam Man was puzzled; he did not understand what I was talking about. I laughed and told him about the lizard. I also thanked him for presenting me with a good solution to my problem of whether or not to share the Buddha's rice grains with the lizard. Brother Tam Man's face brightened.

"If that's what you intend to do," he said, "why not leave some extra grains of rice at the foot of the bowl every time the offering is made to the Buddha? Then your little lizard will take those grains that are intended for him and won't disturb the Buddha's bowl." It was a great suggestion. Excited with this solution, we joined hands but didn't dare to laugh out loud as it might have disturbed the quietness of the resting period in the temple.

Yesterday after the midday meal I took Brother Man's hand and told him the bad news. Our lizard had died.

"While I was lighting the incense," I told him, "I heard a 'thump!' on the stone floor. When I went to look, I saw our lizard lying there dead."

"How can you be so sure it's our lizard?" Brother Tam Man asked.

"Why not?" I replied. "Until yesterday he came every day to get the rice. But today the few grains left at the foot of the bowl were still there."

Brother Tam Man consoled me. "Dear Brother, I'm sure that once the lizard knew how to eat rice, he stopped eating ants or termites or other insects. This means that he didn't create bad karma by killing other creatures, and he was able to have some of the Buddha's rice. He will reach nirvana. We will pray for him."

It made me think about the life span of a living being. Small and fragile as a bubble on a vast ocean, it sinks and disappears into forgetfulness for a thousand lifetimes. Absorbed in my abstract thinking, I was slow to reply to Tam Man's words: "Yes, we will pray for him."

AUNTIE TU

No one knew exactly when and from where Auntie Tu came. It was said that she came to the temple a long time ago, before the time of the present preceptor and abbot. She was very old, perhaps over sixty. She only had a few teeth left but was in very good health. She shared a little hut near the goat house with Auntie Bang. Together these two aunts took care of the cooking for the community. Auntie Bang's nature was more difficult and so we were not as close to her as we were to Auntie Tu, who was always smiling. She loved us dearly. If Brother Man and I had any good stories, we would always share them with her. She would always offer us her easy-going smile that was full of gentleness. When she laughed, her eyes would all but disappear into the crevices of her face. She could neither read nor write Vietnamese and Brother Man tried to persuade her as sweetly as he could to learn it, but she was determined not to.

"What good is it to learn a foreign language now? I'm too old. It's you who needs to study hard so that you will be of service to the Dharma."

Brother Man laughed. "No one is asking you to learn a foreign language, Auntie. We want to encourage you to learn our mother tongue." But Auntie would have nothing to do with it. She could not believe that the words written with a metallic nibbed pen could be our language. For Aunt Tu, our language was *an nam* (classical Vietnamese written in Chinese characters) and it was written with a brush.

As for the Sino-Vietnamese language, Auntie knew bits and pieces — she could follow along when we read, for example, the Ten Directions, With One-Pointed Mind, or Going for Refuge chants. Her practice was very diligent. There was not a single session of the practice of Pure Land chanting that she missed. When the time for the chanting approached, she would put aside her work in the kitchen and wash her hands and face. Auntie wore an oversized gray robe, around her neck hung a black beaded rosary, and on her feet she wore a clopping pair of wooden sandals. She would drag her sandals as she walked from the kitchen to the landing where the bell was, and from there Auntie would go barefoot into the Buddha

Hall and squeeze herself into a corner to wait for the Sangha to come up to the hall for the service.

Auntie really loved to learn the sutras. She had learned by heart the Pure Land chant and the Bowing Deeply before the Buddha and Going for Refuge chants. She wanted to learn by heart the Surangama Dharani mantra, but Brother Man and I doubted that she could handle it because it was five to six times longer than the Mantra of Great Compassion. She was getting old and her mind was already becoming forgetful; how would it be possible for her to learn it by heart! Yet she was so thirsty to learn and so sincere in her desire that we had to give in to her. So Brother Man made a notebook for her from a stack of gold and silver paper that he bound together, and I made a cover from two pieces of cardboard that were painted brown. Beginning with the words from the introduction to the Dharani, I wrote several lines in the notebook in very large print, each word as large as a matchbox.

"Beginning from today," I told her, "Brother Man will give you a sentence a day to learn. If you are diligent then perhaps in five months you will be able to memorize this sutra."

Her eyes squinted as she smiled, exposing her broken teeth in a cute way. "If I can't do it in five months, I'll do it in seven months," she announced. "If I can't do it in seven months, I'll do it in a year. Don't worry about me not being able to learn."

And with that she began to study. Brother Man continued to give her lessons for three or four days. Then on the fifth day, when he was ready to give a new lesson, I gave her a test on the lessons she had already learned. Caught off guard by this unexpected quiz, Auntie could not remember the sentences she had already learned.

"This won't do," I told her. "If you study like this there's no way you'll be able to learn the Surangama Dharani by heart. Each time you learn new lessons you forget the old ones, and if you go over the old lessons you will forget the new ones."

"Then, Brother, if you know of a way to help me memorize my lessons, please tell me."

"Let's do it this way," I suggested. "Study a few verses at a time, and each day we will give you a test. If you pass the test you can go on to some new verses; if you don't pass the test, then you have to go back to the old lesson. We'll have a complete review every three days. Do you agree?"

"I agree," Aunt Tu said.

"Then today let's start from the beginning," I said. "And," I added, "there will be a penalty each time you don't pass the test."

"A penalty?" Aunt Tu asked. But she consented immediately. "All right, a penalty is okay," she said. "If I know there's a penalty, I'll put extra effort into my study. But how are you two going to punish me? I'm not able to kneel for as long as an incense stick burns down — my knees are too weak."

I laughed. "No one would ever make you kneel like that. We'll think of something else."

Auntie also laughed and as she returned to her work she said, "Dear Brothers, please think about it."

I tried to remember the different ways we had been punished at school — like detention, or having to copy our lessons by hand, or sweeping the classroom floor, when suddenly Brother Man burst out laughing.

"Shh, quiet, Brother Man," I reprimanded. "Don't laugh so loud. We'll get into trouble if our teachers hear you. We should take our study seriously."

Brother Man tried to restrain himself, but he just had to tell me what made him laugh.

"I just thought of the perfect penalty," he explained.

"What is it?" I asked. "Let's hear it."

"Each time Aunt Tu doesn't pass the quiz, she has to give both of us four squares of fried tofu for lunch," he replied.

Our temple was very poor, so our everyday meals were modest. Just two squares of tofu would have been precious enough; four squares reserved especially for us would be a rare and wonderful thing! Yes, having a meal with fried tofu would be perfect — and Aunt Tu, who was in charge of shopping for groceries and cooking our meals, was capable of providing those perfect meals for us.

I agreed, and we immediately went to tell Aunt Tu. She nearly fell over laughing when she heard our proposal.

"That's it," I announced happily. "That's the penalty."

The penalty was very agreeable to us. Auntie Tu was also okay with it. And that was how once in a while we were able to enjoy delicious pieces of tofu with our lunch. Sometimes Brother Man, who was younger, couldn't contain himself and would giggle while eating his tofu. I wanted to laugh too, but being older, I pretended to be more serious. "Now Brother Man, you're not meditating on the Five Contemplations or you wouldn't always be laughing!"

There came a time, however, when Auntie always recited her lessons correctly, and because there was no penalty we were not getting any tofu on our lunch trays. During one lunch I complained to Brother Man, "It's been a while since we've had any tofu, Brother." He leaned close to me and whispered something into my ear. I nodded and smiled in agreement.

That evening, instead of the usual two verses, Brother Man gave Aunt Tu four verses to study. It was so much to memorize, I was sure she would get a penalty the next day. At noon the following day, I went to the kitchen to borrow a knife to cut paper for a bookbinding project and I saw Aunt Tu lean-

ing against the wall, nodding off to sleep with the sutra in her hand. She woke as I entered and hurriedly sat up.

"Why don't you take a nap?" I asked her. "Go rest, so you can work later. We're all going out to look for more wood this afternoon, right, Auntie?"

Aunt Tu answered softly. "I have to study so I can recite these verses by heart," she said. "If I don't, Brother Man will punish me. That would be very bad!"

"Not that bad," I smiled. "You'd just have to fry some tofu."

She motioned for me to come closer. Then she lowered her voice.

"Frying tofu is not a problem," she whispered. "But lately the treasurer of our temple has cut back our grocery allowance. This year our rice field didn't yield a good crop. Our daily allowance isn't even enough to buy vegetables for the Sangha. Where can I find money to buy tofu?"

"So you're studying hard to avoid getting the penalty, aren't you?" I asked.

She gave a sad nod. But then she smiled again. Listening to her and watching her smile, I felt some remorse. Poor Aunt Tu, I loved her so much.

"Brother Man and I will not enforce the tofu penalty from now on," I assured her. "We'll find another kind of penalty.

From now on you won't have to fry any tofu for us. Go, Auntie, put your sutra book away and go rest. You are tired."

She happily agreed.

I went straight to Brother Man's room, and told him very quietly what had just happened. Then I gently put my finger on his forehead: "This was because of you!" I said.

His look was slightly reproachful as he replied, "And who forced you to agree with me?"

THE KOAN

Brother Man would often ask me to explain stories from the book *The Gateless Gate*. Although I was several years ahead of him at the Institute of Buddhist Studies, I still found it impossible to explain those stories. I didn't think that they would mean anything to people who were not in the stories because they did not share the same circumstances. I told Brother Man to think about the words "gateless gate" — they were already meaningless.

"How can I explain 'the gate that is not a gate'?" I asked him.

"But the author wouldn't have just written meaningless stories." Brother Man seemed a little annoyed.

"I think the author did write meaningless stories. 'Meaningful' means 'meaningful to someone,' it doesn't mean 'meaningful to everyone.' So it may mean nothing to a person who did not find himself in the same circumstances. But for someone who is in those circumstances, it is meaningful."

Brother Man was not happy with my explanation. He smiled at me, but it was a sarcastic smile, one that showed he thought I was quibbling. That made me angry, and I didn't speak to him during lunch that day.

The next day when I went to pick jackfruit for soup, I took the opportunity to invite Brother Man along in order for us to make up. I asked his help to climb a jackfruit tree that was in the pineapple garden. We needed to pick a young fresh jackfruit. Taking a knife, a basket, and the jackfruit, we then went down to the crescent-moon-shaped pond that was in front of the temple. There we sat on the edge of the pond, four legs dangling in the water. Wetting the knife, I began to peel the fruit and opened a conversation.

"Do you know why it is that when we first entered the monastery we were not allowed to study the teachings right away but had to go through heavy manual work for a long time?"

Brother Man reflected a moment then replied, "Because our teacher wanted us to pass through a testing period to see whether our aspiration was strong enough. If we had become dispirited during this period, it would have meant that we didn't have the capacity to pursue the practice of Zen."

I dipped the half-peeled jackfruit into the water so that its sap didn't stick to the knife, then said, "That's possible. But I think there's another reason."

"It's probably because we follow the Zen principle of 'no work, no food'— if we don't work, then we don't eat — and we have to learn this as soon as we enter the monastery."

I burst out laughing. "That explanation is even worse than the first one. In my opinion, the initial working period is necessary so that the master can understand the level of our practice and our aptitude. Only when there's a deep understanding of the disciple's mentality can the master know what teachings to give his disciple. The teaching that the master then gives to the disciple is for him alone; only he can receive what the teacher is trying to transmit in its full sense. That was why yesterday I said that what a Zen master says can only be meaningful to the person he is talking to."

Brother Man's eyes lit up. "I can see it very clearly now. In *The Gateless Gate* there is a story about a disciple who, when he arrived at the monastery, went to pay his respects to his teacher and to ask for a teaching. The teacher asked him, 'Have you had your breakfast yet?' The disciple replied, 'Yes teacher, I have.' The teacher then said, 'Then go and wash your bowl.' The way I see it, the teacher's comments had two meanings. The first is that the disciple needed to take the first steps but not to rush, so that the master had time to understand him. The second meaning is that the disciple had to see that the business of washing his bowl was the first task of practicing Zen."

"I agree, Brother. We can understand the meaning of this story because you and I have been in the same situation as this disciple. We know from our own experience that the comment 'Then go and wash your bowl' is a suitable teaching."

I remember very clearly how lost I felt when I first came to the monastery; it was so different from the ordinary world. The atmosphere was silent and at the same time energetic, solemn but also gentle. On first entering a monastery, a person sees everyone else there as leisurely, upright, gentle, and joyful in a solemn manner. It makes the person feel even more clumsy. If a dieu were to bang a door shut just once, for example, he would be reprimanded right away. We learned and practiced mindful manners by observing and listening to our elders. We learned by watching the way the brother who cared for the altar opened and closed the door with gentle, slow movements when he went out of his room, as though he were afraid of causing unnecessary noise in the monastery.

We examined our actions, language, and thoughts while we were walking, standing, sitting, or lying down. We ourselves became aware of our every move — body, speech, and mind.

Novices could learn all of this from the manual of *Fine Manners,* the second volume of the *Lesser Vinaya.* According to its teaching, every time we moved our body, we allowed a wholesome thought to arise in our mind in order that our movement would be right action. If we do this throughout the day, we will always dwell in mindfulness. For example, when we first wake up in the morning we let the thought arise, "I pray that all beings will have enough wisdom and awakening to penetrate the Ten Directions." Then, when we hear the morning bells we let arise in our mind another good thought. When we get out of bed and our feet search for our slippers, we contemplate the following: "From morning till night, all little beings look after yourselves. If unluckily by accident I step on you, I pray that you will be reborn in the Pure Land." I was very moved when I recited these verses; I saw that both mindfulness and loving kindness were being nourished in me.

When we changed our robes, fastened buttons, tied strings, washed our hands and feet, washed our bowls, swept the ground, went to the bathroom — in other words, no matter what we did — there was a mindful thought that went along with the action. When we washed our hands we reflected on the saying, "When ladling water to wash my hands, I pray that everyone will have pure hands in order to maintain the teachings." When seeing running water, we let arise the wish that everyone will be able to flow in the stream of the true Dharma towards the fruit of Buddhahood. The contemplation we used when we went to the bathroom was, "May all beings be free from anger, greed, and delusion and from all wrongdoings."

Auntie Tu really liked the verse, "Sweeping the ground of the monastery diligently makes happiness and understanding arise." She would often recite it when she swept the fallen leaves in front of the temple. It means that diligently sweeping the temple grounds can increase merit, virtue, and wisdom.

In summary, the book *Fine Manners* teaches novices to manage their thoughts so that their minds don't wander off like a monkey jumping from branch to branch or like a horse breaking out of its corral. Once they are able to practice these verses from the book, they are able to create new verses along the same lines. Brother Man and I often discussed this, and I suggested writing another whole book of verses for the practice. For example, when closing a book we could let arise, "When closing a book, may I reshape any carelessness and crookedness in my spiritual life." Surely there would need to be a verse for getting on an airplane. In the past no novices traveled by airplane, so there were no verses for it. I told

Brother Man that if I ever got to fly to Nha Trang, I would say, "Stepping onto an airplane, may all beings achieve the power to quickly fly back to the shore of liberation." We both laughed loudly.

Brother Man helped me wash the jackfruit clean of the sap and we gathered the skin to throw under the pepper tree.

"When we first enter a monastery," I continued, "the responsibility of a disciple is to know how to look and how to listen in order to see the way in which the high monks walk, stand, lie down, sit, work, and meditate. They have been through the training and their body, speech, and mind are by now adorned with at least some fine manners that make them peaceful and easy to respect. You have studied the *Fine Manners* so you must know how a novice must train body and mind in such a way so as to develop a spiritual life. A person who has joined the meditation school must also know how to listen to the exceptionally original language of the Zen tradition. This language is not just a language of sounds but also that of body actions. It might turn out to be a startling language that could shake the foundation of one's entire lifetime, destroy a world view, strip away an existing form. Brother, do you remember the story of Master Chao-Chou's dog?"

"No, I don't remember it."

"A disciple went to ask the master, 'Respected teacher, does a dog have Buddha nature?'

"The master replied: 'Yes.'

"The next day another disciple went to ask the same question, 'Respected teacher, does a dog have Buddha nature?'

"The master replied: 'No.'"

Brother Tam Man replied, "Since there were two different aptitudes, the teachings given by the master were different. The truth doesn't lie either in the words 'yes' or 'no' but in the way the master deals with the disciple and opens up his or her understanding, right, Brother?"

"That is absolutely right. 'Yes' or 'no' here were not the truth, but were just a means to point to the truth. In Buddhism, this is called 'the explanation depending on the person.' It's a koan that is understood only by the person who asked the question. In the first instance, the disciple asked with a sincere desire to understand and not to be caught, therefore the master replied 'yes.' In the second instance, the one who asked was probably someone who enjoyed discussing theories and made it into a dogma; therefore the response was 'no.' This 'no' most likely shook the one asking the question in a way that he did not know which direction to take because for so long he had worshipped that 'yes' like a star that guided his path. But then we, too, are observing from the outside; we cannot understand the effect of the two words 'yes' and 'no' in the same way that the two disciples of Master Chao-Chou did."

"I see that in books on Zen there is often condemnation for theory and debate," Brother Man added. "Working, looking, and listening are the most important things for someone who is learning and practicing Zen, and not discussion about the ultimate."

I nodded in agreement. "That is the reason we study *The Essential Vinaya for Daily Use* and *Fine Manners* when we are working. We need to bind our body and mind together in a stable discipline before we can hope to practice Zen. Just think, Brother, the Zen practitioner trains himself to be concentrated in order to practice meditation in the same way that a scientist follows the discipline of the laboratory in order to do an experiment. For example, while carrying firewood from the mountains, your practice is to focus your thoughts on the act of carrying wood; you do not allow your mind to think about anything else, like washing clothes, grinding rice, and so forth. Another method is to look at a glass of water that is three or four yards away from you and concentrate your mind on that glass for ten to thirty minutes. Practicing like this, your concentration will get stronger and stronger every day, and when your concentration is strong, meditation becomes easy. Not only do you develop your concentration, but you develop your ability to look deeply and to be more creative. Once you know how to focus your mind with the energy of meditative concentration, other things will come more easily too; for example, if you are studying geometry, you will be able to find solutions very quickly."

When we returned to the temple, I brought the jackfruit to Auntie Tu in the kitchen and she cut it into thin strips to make soup. Brother Man and I then went to the mountains to pick some herbs that are essential for making a good jackfruit soup. *San* is a thorny mountain herb that has pinkish leaves. This herb adds a very nice fragrance and taste to the soup when the leaves are cut up and put into the pot after the jackfruit has cooked. Jackfruit soup was one of the vegetarian dishes that I could cook well, and so I taught Brother Man how to make it, too.

We continued our conversation. "Once the master sees that his disciples are well-trained," I said, "and that each has some concentration energy, he will begin to teach each one in a way that is suited to his unique nature. The disciple also receives a koan to meditate on, such as, 'All dharmas go to One, but where will One go?' Once the disciple receives a koan, he'll have to live with it day and night until he reaches an awakened state [*satori* in Japanese]. Receiving a koan is not a theoretical way to study; it is like an arrow being shot deeply into the student's shoulder that makes him agonize day and night. Every moment the practitioner focuses on that koan as an object of meditation, looking deeply with his whole conscious and subconscious mind."

Brother Tam Man asked, "Does that mean the practitioner has to meditate on the koan with each action, while eating, drinking, sitting, standing, walking, and lying down?"

"Precisely. But you must not think, Brother, that this effort to understand uses the reasoning mind. Rather, the practitioner focuses his mind on one thing, each action, in order to silence the disorder of the mind. You have studied Buddhist psychology so you already know that the way of reasoning separates one thing from everything else by creating concepts, which in turn obscure things. It is called 'imaginary construction' in Buddhist psychology. We must find a different way of understanding — the kind of understanding derived from meditation — which can arise thanks to the power of concentration. When we are focused on one object, our mind is no longer dispersed, and because it is not dispersed, concentration is developed. It is this concentration that is active, not only in the consciousness but also in the *alaya* — our store consciousness. Even while we are sleeping, concentration and the store consciousness continue to work. The store consciousness is like a big pot used to cook these koans, and the fire is the ability to meditate and concentrate. When the koan has been cooked, then quite naturally, thanks to favorable conditions being present, it manifests the truth fully on the surface of our conscious mind. And this is called enlightenment."

Brother Man nodded his head. "I know that the store consciousness must be busy even when we are asleep. When yesterday afternoon I went into town to buy a book, I met a person I knew on the street. He greeted me, but I couldn't remember his name. Perhaps I couldn't remember it because it has been such a long since I have seen him. When I left him and continued down the street, I tried hard to recall his name in my consciousness; it made my head ache, but still I couldn't remember his name. Later I completely forgot about the incident. This morning while I was brushing my teeth, when I wasn't thinking about anything, suddenly his name came back to me without any effort."

"So who was it, Brother?"

"It was Binh, the man we met when we were evacuating. Do you remember, Brother, we met him when we were trying to find some salt to buy?"

"Yes, I haven't seen him for a long time, either. Your story, Brother Man, has made me remember something funny that happened to me when I was about eight years old. In our front yard, behind a screen, we kept a big jar container that held rainwater; the rim of the jar came up to my chest. I liked to play with this water. One day, I saw some yellow leaves at the bottom of the jar and I wanted to take them out. So I rolled up my sleeves all the way to my shoulders and put my arm into the jar, but my arm was too short to touch the bottom. So I found a stick, cleaned it, and tried to pierce the leaves with the stick — but it didn't work because the end of the stick wasn't sharp enough. Annoyed, I began to stir the water with the stick instead. I was hoping that stirring it would get the leaves to float up to the top, but after about twenty or thirty swirls they still wouldn't rise, so I gave up and walked away. Moments later I returned, and to my surprise I saw that the leaves had floated up to the surface on their own. It turned out that after I stopped stirring, the water in the jar continued to swirl, and the leaves rose to the surface."

Brother Man laughed and said, "So you picked the leaves out and threw them away."

"Naturally," I said as I laughed with him. "You see, what we are talking about is the same. Even when we are not meditating, if we remain focused, the work of our mind still has the energy to cook the koan in our store consciousness. During sitting meditation we learn how to be mindful of our breath and our body; and during our daily activities, we focus our mind on what we are doing."

"How long does it take for us to cook a koan, Brother?"

"That depends on the ability and effort of the practitioner. There are those who get enlightened quickly and those who take much longer. Let me tell you a story about someone who took a long time to get enlightened. There was a Chinese Zen master who had many disciples. After twenty years, all but one became enlightened and were sent to faraway lands to transmit the teachings. This one disciple, however, after many years of study and much practice still hadn't broken open the shell of ignorance to attain enlightenment. He was very ashamed, and because of this he tried even harder. The master never showed any signs of impatience with him. That winter the disciple and the master were living alone in a cave in the mountains.

"One night during winter there was a snowstorm in the mountains where they were living in a cave. That morning the fallen snow was so deep that it covered the entrance of the cave. It was very cold and the master told his disciple to go find wood for the fire. But the path outside the cave was fully covered in snow, and so the disciple searched inside the cave for some wood, but none could be found. The master pretended to be upset: 'You must find anything that is made of wood, anything!' he shouted. After another search, the disciple still could not find any wood in the cave; the table and seats, everything was made of stone. 'Respected teacher, there is nothing made of wood,' he said. The master pretended to be even more irritated. 'Then go look in the shrine room,' he yelled. Frightened, the disciple went into the shrine room, but he still couldn't see anything made of wood, other than the statue of the Buddha on a jade table. Shaking, he reported back to his master, 'Respected teacher, there is only the wooden statue of the Buddha.' The master shouted, 'I said anything made of wood!' Never before had the disciple seen his master angry, and the frightened disciple was shaking when he brought the wooden statue to the master. Then, in front of the utterly surprised disciple, the master took an axe and split the Buddha statue into four pieces and threw each piece into the fire and watched as it caught fire.

"Do you know what happened, Brother? It shook the disciple dumb; and suddenly he saw his mind clear and break through the veil of ignorance. The thick shell was finally smashed to pieces and the light of enlightenment was allowed in. I'm sure that the disciple's mind had been readied for this; by then there was only a small blockage that prevented enlightenment. The master had waited for the right moment to tip the scales and destroy the last obstacle."

"It is like a jack-in-the-box," Brother Man said. "The springs and toy man in the box are ready, all that is needed is for the button to be pressed and the puppet will pop out."

"It's just like that. A Zen master follows his disciple closely. That's why the time a disciple spends working with his teacher is the link. When the teacher sees the aptitude of the disciple, he will transmit a koan. And when it is necessary to bring down the guillotine on him, he does not hesitate to do so. Usually these guillotines are successful. But there have been times when the master did not thoroughly understand the aptitude of his disciple and he failed.

"Let me tell you the story about a case where the master was successful. The disciple was a very diligent student; he was always present for meditation sessions and his master's Dharma talks. He was also very intelligent. Sometimes he would imitate his master when he spoke by raising one finger in the manner of a Zen master who is about to say something important. One day when he was attending to his master, he completely forgot himself and solemnly raised one finger as he was about to speak. Seeing this, the master picked up a paper-cutting knife and, grabbing his disciple's hand, cut off the finger that was raised in the air. In agony the disciple screamed and ran off, and the master ran after him. As the master chased after the student he called out, 'Disciple!' The disciple turned to look, and he saw that the master had raised one finger. The disciple also raised one finger, but suddenly he saw that his finger was missing. That's when he became enlightened, and he bowed his head in deep reverence to his master. Do you think that was a true story?"

Brother Man replied, "I think that was too violent."

"There were even more violent examples than that one. But the importance lies in the enlightenment. Let me tell you of a case in which the master was not successful. There was a disciple who had been contemplating for a long time on a koan but was still not enlightened. He was very ashamed. The master said to him, 'Return in three months.' Three months later there were still no results. 'Return in three weeks,' the master told him. Three weeks passed and he still was not enlightened. 'Return in three days,' the master said, 'and if by then you're not awakened you might as well die — what's the use of practicing?' Three days later the disciple returned. The master asked, 'Where have you got with the koan?' 'Respected teacher,' he answered, 'I am very ashamed, I still haven't solved it; I will kill myself.' The master shouted loudly. The disciple took out a knife and in a flash he pierced his stomach and fell to the ground. The master looked intently into the face of the dying disciple and asked, 'You have succeeded in suicide, but has the koan been understood?' Breathing with difficulty, the disciple replied, 'Respected teacher, no.' Then the master shot him, saying, 'Quiet, a dead person does not speak.' But not even that final bullet achieved its aim."

"That is a very tragic story," Brother Man said, "I feel a lot of compassion for that disciple, but I know the master must have suffered even more."

"Even so, usually the Zen masters are successful. Just read *Records of High Monks* and *The Gateless Gate* to the very end and you will see. But now the jackfruit is already cooked and we still haven't brought back the fragrant herbs. If we continue to talk like this where is it going to get us, Brother Man?"

When we got back to the kitchen, Auntie Tu was waiting patiently. "You young brothers play too much," she said softly. "The jackfruit soup has been finished for a while now, but there were no herbs to add to it."

A Drop of Nectar

Just one drop of nectar falling from the willow branch,
Puts out the burning fire in the heart of beings in the lower realms.
— Nguyen Du

Vinh came to see me the day I got back from Bao Quoc Buddhist Institute. He brought me a pile of Buddhist books written in French that he had ordered from outside the country. He also had a new edition of a French-Vietnamese dictionary for Brother Tam Man, who was studying French.

Offering the dictionary to Brother Man, Vinh smiled and said, "Your French has improved a lot. You can even read Alphonse Daudet's stories without using a dictionary, right?" Then he added, "My Chinese is still very bad. I'm so forgetful,

I can't remember what I studied. I don't know when I'll be able to read Chinese scriptures as well as you two."

Smiling back, I told Vinh, "Don't worry. You're so smart, if you just use the studying method I showed you, you will surpass even Brother Man in no time."

While I was still living at the root temple, before I left to study at the Buddhist Institute, Vinh studied Chinese with me twice a week. Within three months, he was able to decipher the Chinese book *Basic Lessons in Elementary Buddhist Studies*. He worked hard to learn Chinese so he could research Buddhism. Even with the Baccalaureate exams to enter college approaching, he continued to study Chinese. "It is not so important to pass or fail the exams," he explained. "But to study Buddhism, I need to know Chinese."

It had been six months since the day we met Vinh. He regarded Brother Man and me even closer than his blood brothers. His face was bright and intelligent and his eyes were gentle and portrayed honesty. He had a happy disposition, a warm voice, and a charming, clear laugh. Vinh was easy to love; anyone who spoke to him would take to him. Brother Man was very close to Vinh — if after a few days Vinh did not visit, Brother Man would ask about him.

Yet, there was a time when Vinh was tired of life, and because of this was determined to "shave his head and become a monk." We got to know him through very special circumstances. That was six months ago, to the day. I wonder if he'll mind me writing his personal story. I don't think he will.

On that day, Linh Quang Temple in Hue held an unexpected assembly of the Thua Thien Province Monastic Congregation, and the abbot and *bhikshus* from the temple left early in the morning to attend. The temple was almost empty; only Brother Man and I were left. I was writing up my studies when Brother Man came to tell me that there was a guest.

"There's a young man asking to see the abbot," he said. "I don't know whether to ask him to stay or not."

I put down my pen and replied, "You can ask him to stay, Brother. Invite him into the guest house. I'll be there in a few moments."

I put on my robe and went to greet him. The young man was looking at a painting of the Bodhisattva Avalokiteshvara. He looked contemplative. Hearing me enter, he turned around and stood up. I invited him to sit and poured him some tea. I asked him if there was anything urgent that needed to be passed on to my teacher. He quickly replied that there was nothing urgent. Then he sat still, quietly observing all the things on display in the guest house. I also sat silently, without asking him further questions. Suddenly he asked, "How long have you been a monk, Brother?"

"I've been a monk for almost three years," I said, looking at him.

"How old were you when you came?"

"Nineteen."

"So this year you are twenty-two years old. I just turned twenty-three," he said. "I'm a little older than you." His voice suddenly became soft and intimate. "You must regard me as your brother," he said, "and not be angry if I ask too many personal questions."

I laughed. "I wouldn't think of it. Please go ahead and ask."

He was quiet for a moment and then he asked, "Why did you become a monk?"

I raised my eyes, looked at him, and felt slightly uncomfortable. But quickly I came back to myself and answered directly, "Because I like Buddhism and its teaching of mindful living. I was born in a Buddhist family and had the chance to read about Buddhism in books and magazines. I found myself naturally drawn to the ideal of liberation in Buddhism and to this lifestyle, especially when I learned it could help us understand reality as it is."

As he listened attentively, I noticed there was some sadness he was trying to hide. Afraid that I would see his sadness, he took a deep breath. Finally, he said quietly, "I have a friend who wants to become a monk, but my friend doesn't know if there are any requirements."

"How old is your friend?" I asked.

"Around the same age as you and me."

"Is your friend still a student?"

"Yes, he has completed the first half of the Baccalaureate Degree. So, Brother, do you know what it takes for my friend to become a monk? What does he need in order to be ordained?"

"About the requirements…" I said, hesitating, "there really aren't that many." Then unexpectedly, I asked, "Has your friend been disappointed in love or something?" My question was so unexpected it embarrassed him. He looked completely bewildered. I felt compassion for him.

"If your friend is disappointed in love," I continued, "he wouldn't be encouraged to ordain."

"Why is that, Brother?"

"Because he would not be able to endure the life of a monk," I replied.

"Why not?" he asked.

"Because he lacks a strong will. He wants to be a monk now because he has been disappointed in love. That is what many people do — having failed in an endeavor, they become weary of life and want to escape it altogether. If a person is disappointed and weary of life, it means a strong will is lacking. And if there is no strong will, how is it possible to live the life of someone who needs to practice perseverance and perhaps endure some hardship?"

"My friend will not be afraid of a life of hardship," he replied.

"It is not physical hardship I'm talking about, it's a strong commitment to withstand trials and be able to make an effort to reach the goal of a spiritual path. If it is because of a disappointment in love that your friend turns to the spiritual path, sooner or later he'll give that up too."

"Please, Brother, say more."

"First of all, your friend would be entering the monastery with a heavy heart and a great sadness. That in itself is not right. While others have entered the monastic life with clarity and a sincere aspiration to take the vows, your friend instead enters the monastery with the intention of escaping and turning away from the world. The practice community is not a refuge for souls saddened by disappointment."

"But doesn't Buddhism help those who are suffering?" he asked.

"That is true. But there are many ways of helping. Those

who do not share the concerns of the Sangha cannot be a part of the Sangha."

"Please tell me what these concerns are."

"As I've said, the purpose is to gain liberation and awakening for oneself and others. In this case, your friend does not have that intention. He only wants to escape life. But the Dharma came into being to live life. To practice as monks is to train ourselves in mindfulness and awakening, to first free ourselves from suffering and then to help others do the same."

"Who knows," Vinh said, "later on my friend might be able to share this aspiration and achieve its goal."

"That's something we can't foretell. But if he entered the monastic life now, he would suffer more than if he remained in the world. We feel free, at peace, and happy, living in a peaceful environment such as this; but your friend, on the other hand, would suffer miserably precisely because of this very peace and quiet. The more solitary the place he lives, the more he'll have to confront his sadness and despair, and the more he will suffer. We enjoy hearing the sound of the bell, and it makes us feel more peaceful and concentrated each time we hear it — whereas for your friend, the sound of the bell would make him feel mournful because his soul is wounded and not as whole as those around him."

It was lunch and Brother Man had just finished the offering to the Buddha. Our young guest expressed regret that we would have to stop our conversation, so I warmly invited him to stay for lunch. His eyes brightened. There were just the three of us at lunch. Brother Man had thoughtfully asked Auntie Tu earlier on to prepare an extra dish of young bamboo shoots and include it in our meal.

After lunch, Vinh (it was at lunchtime that we finally learned his name) wanted to continue our talk. The three of us walked out to the hills and sat down under a row of pine trees. I introduced Brother Man to Vinh. Together we talked with Vinh as though we had known him for a long time.

He asked us, "Have you read *An Afternoon Went By* by Nhat Linh?"

"Yes, I have," I said. "Your mentioning this book must mean you have understood what I told you this morning. The nun in Nhat Linh's book became a nun because she had been disappointed in love. Living in a peaceful environment, hearing the bells, she never felt a bit at ease. It was the opposite for her — she suffered even more, she became more broken. Therefore, when she left the monastery with a visitor, it wasn't surprising. Luckily she was just a character in a novel. We do not want people like this in the monastery."

Unintentionally, my words made Vinh blush. He turned away and pretended to look in the direction of the temple tower. But Brother Man was quick to see his embarrassment and tried to lighten things up. "It might be evening before the elder brothers return," he said.

Vinh suddenly turned back towards us and said, "Then my friend shouldn't ordain?"

"Right, he really shouldn't," I replied. "He should try to free himself from the shell of his clouded mind that he's been caught in. Life is beautiful but your friend does not see it. Look at us — we enjoy our life as monks, we have our aspirations and a spiritual path. We want to live our ideal. There are only two things we try to avoid — we want to free ourselves from craving and delusion. Your friend should free himself from his broken heart, and the sooner the better. That will help the deepest and most wholesome aspirations in him to manifest."

Brother Man smiled and asked Vinh, "To want to be a monk just because someone betrayed you, do you think that is a good motivation?"

Vinh replied, softly, "Shouldn't we at least feel some compassion for him?"

"Yes, of course, we should feel compassion for him."

"If my friend would no longer want to ordain but only wanted to learn about the monastic life, is it still a bad idea, Brother Man?"

"That, you'll need to ask Brother Quan."

"Of course it's not bad. Quite the opposite, we would sympathize with him. And if he would like to come to the monastery from time to time to learn more about the Dharma and to participate in the practice, we would be delighted," I replied.

Vinh laughed, joyfully. "Then for sure I'll bring my friend along. He'll probably love you brothers."

Two days later Vinh returned, but he came alone. It turned out that his friend and himself were the same person. He looked fresher and younger than he had looked on the previous visit.

"Thanks, Brother," he said, "for liberating me from a dark situation. Your words as well as your way of being relieved my sorrow and the weariness I felt. When I returned home that day, I thought a lot about what you had said. I saw that I was almost drowning in my darkness. My encounter with you brought about much healing. I feel lighter now. I can study and I can smile again. I have rediscovered the joy of living."

"But I still doubt that you have completely healed."

"Yes, but I can say I am on the way to total recovery. You do not know how much I was suffering in the past two months."

"But now you have benefited from a few drops of the

compassionate nectar of the Dharma. I hope you have a chance to study and practice the Dharma and discover more about the beauty and depth of this path of compassion."

"I would like to learn more about Buddhism. For a long time, I had many wrong views — I thought Buddhism was a place for the sorrowful and weary soul. I would like to go deeper, but to do so, I have to study Chinese."

I encouraged him to study Chinese and promised to help him. From then on, he began coming to the temple twice a week. During our rest time, we'd go and spend time out in the hills. I told Vinh about the history of Buddhism and its contributions in shaping the culture of Vietnam. He listened, mesmerized by stories of the prosperous period of the Ly and Tran dynasties when Buddhism prospered to everyone's advantage, and he developed his own ideas on ways to rebuild a program of Buddhist studies for the nation.

"One day," he said, "perhaps I will also ordain. But for now I need to exert my strong will to learn the basics of Buddhism. I hope that in the future I will have the ability to be of service to this path. It makes me happy to see that you brothers carry in you so many positive seeds for the future of Buddhist monasticism. The Sangha must rediscover the vitality of the Ly and Tran dynasties."

Currently Vinh is very accomplished in classical Chinese. He recently sent me a piece he had translated from a review of the *Voice of Understanding*. He wrote that he still has one more year of university studies and then he will be able to devote all of his time to research Buddhism. Who would have guessed that this young man needed only one drop of the Dharma's nectar of compassion to be reborn into a joyful life?

RETURN

My teacher used to tell us stories, his voice full of deep respect, about the patriarchs of our temple. Nhat Dinh, a venerable monk who lived over a hundred years ago, was the Zen master who originally founded the Tu Hieu Meditation school and our root temple. My teacher told us this story about him that had been passed down over the years.

Long ago, the patriarch went up to Spring of Yang Hill near to where the temple tombs are now located, chose a peaceful spot to clear, and built a hermitage where he could practice and take care of his aging mother. In this hermitage, which he named "Nourishing Peace," he followed the Buddha's teachings faithfully. His concentration was very deep and he wasn't caught in anything small or petty.

Even though he was a Zen master, he cared for the needs of his old mother. When living in an era where there is no Buddha, taking care of one's parents is as virtuous and meritorious as taking care of the Buddha. One time his mother was ill and needed some nourishing food to recover. Knowing that in the past his mother liked to eat rice soup with fresh fish, he went to the market to buy a fish to prepare for his mother. People were shocked to see a monk buying a fish and carrying it home, but they dared not say anything to him, knowing that he was a high monk and could do no wrong. People didn't understand it, however, and they gossiped about him behind his back. But the master continued to be himself in his natural, unaffected way as he walked through the streets carrying a fish home from the market. He knew what he was doing and he did not get caught in other people's opinions of him, which were based on their ignorance.

When I first heard this story I felt a joy that almost brought me to tears. Nhat Dinh demonstrated a free and liberated attitude that wasn't bound by dogma — like a poem that a person who is caught in prejudices would never be able to live or understand. Later on, Nourishing Peace Hermitage grew into a large temple and King Tu Duc, who was very dedicated to his own mother, gave it the name the "Imperially-Appointed Temple of Loving Kindness and Filial Love." The master passed away in the tenth lunar month of the year 1847.

My teacher also told us a story about Patriarch Hai Thieu,

whom he was fortunate to have met. The venerable Hai Thieu was a well-known Zen master who made fifteen great vows that have been engraved on a memorial stone in front of his stupa. His portrait, which is still with us, shows him with beautiful long, thick eyebrows. When he was aging, his eyelids drooped over his eyes like two blinds covering a window. Whenever he wanted to look at something he had to lift his eyelids with his hand in order to see. Then he'd pull them down again to close his eyes. But he rarely lifted his eyelids, since hearing was enough for him. On the occasion when someone returned after being away for some time, he would lift his eyelids and look clearly into the face of the traveler before calling a novice to offer the guest some tea.

Once a young dieu called Phuoc disobeyed the master. This dieu was just eight years old and somewhat mischievous. The master told the dieu to find a cane with which to swat him. Dieu Phuoc knew that the master couldn't see, so after lying down to be swatted, he rolled to one side when the cane came down so that the cane missed him and hit the mattress. The master hit twice, and both times the dieu managed to avoid being struck. Not realizing this, the master told the dieu to put away the cane and advised him not to be disobedient again.

That evening Phuoc developed a fever. Even with medicine, the fever continued for three days. When asked, the dieu admitted what he had done to avoid the master's punishment. The behavior of the dieu so shocked one of the novices that he put on his long robe and went to pay his respect to the master. He told the master exactly what had happened and requested that the master pardon the boy. Upon hearing the story, the master said, "Is that so?" and then told the novice to make some rice soup for the boy to eat. The monk did as the master requested, and after eating the rice soup, Dieu Phuoc began to get better. From that time on everyone feared the severity and virtue of the master.

I said to Auntie Tu, "It doesn't make sense that a master who was so compassionate would punish a young child by inflicting a fever on him just because the child was foolish."

"Of course not, young Brother," she replied. "The master didn't know about the foolish behavior of the dieu, so how could he punish him for it? It was because Dieu Phuoc offended the master's great virtue that the Dharma protectors punished him."

I believed that the master's virtue had been offended, but not that the Dharma protectors were punishing him. I thought surely the Dharma protectors would not be so immature as to punish a young child of eight. I did think, however, that the boundless and unseen energy of the master's consciousness and spiritual practice was enough to cause such an event to happen.

One blazing hot afternoon, King Thanh Thai came to visit the master at the temple. The king stopped on the road, and leaving his carriages with the attendants, walked half a kilometer over the pine hill to the temple. All the monks were out that day and the aunts had already returned to their hut. The young dieu and novices were working in the back garden and were not aware of the king's arrival.

The king entered the gate alone and went to the lotus pond along the path that led to the dining hall. He entered Enjoying Faithfulness Hall, and seeing it was deserted, he walked quietly towards the master's quarters. The master was sitting in meditation on a low bed made of planks held up by four curved feet. The master did not see the king enter. The king sat down on the floor at the master's feet, and after a while he gently placed his hands on the master's knees. The master asked, "Who's there?"

The king replied "Respected teacher, I am the king here to visit you."

The master smiled and reached out to take the king's hand. He said softly, "Oh, the king is here. Your Majesty, please sit down. Let me call a dieu to bring you some cassava to eat."

Around three in the afternoon the aunts usually cooked a pot of cassava and sweet potatoes for the dieus and novices. This simple snack was given to all those who had to work in the afternoon before going out into the garden. The aunts would often choose the softest potato and put it on a plate to offer to the venerable.

The spirit of veneration shown by King Thanh Thai was worthy of esteem, but the attitude towards high officials shown by the master was even worthier of esteem. There is truthfully nothing more democratic than the image of a king visiting a monk and being invited by the monk to share his simple dish. This story was retold in a very down-to-earth manner by the master to his students, where my teacher heard it firsthand. We heard it through oral transmission from our teacher.

On the topic of equality and democracy in Buddhism, Brother Man and I were delighted to see that these qualities that were so valued in the world were also part of Buddhism. In fact, there is no other tradition that encourages people to see themselves as equal to its leaders in respect to their innate nature and potential. The Buddha was a fully-enlightened person, not a god, who had the ability to show the way to people in his society. A spiritual path based on the teachings of interbeing, interdependent arising, and interdependent causation — where individuals determine their own future and take responsibility for their actions, whether they be constructive or destructive — truly suits the spirit of democracy in modern society. The happiness of the individual depends on the individual's own actions. Furthermore, the spirit of free inquiry is the most precious thing about Buddhism. Buddhism does not tolerate dictatorial thinking — the intellect aims at eliminating prejudices and fanaticism. You can read the sutras and commentaries and make new spiritual discoveries without fear of being condemned or excommunicated by any power, even that of the congregation. When a devotee prostrates to a high monk it is not out of obedience to any rules, regulations, authority, or ritual; it comes from a fondness and respect for the virtues of the monk.

You can write books to explain your discoveries, and even create a new school if your discovery is truly able to revive a vital pulse of Buddhism. Even if your theory conflicts with existing contemporary theories, no one has the power to condemn or expel you. Because of this tolerance, the garden of literature and philosophy in Buddhism is exceptionally rich. There are a hundred thousand different fragrant flowers and plants. When you examine the matter carefully, you will find that only the deepest and most genuine discoveries have been Buddhism's life breath. Abstract theories can never take root in the garden of Buddhism. Although there may be ten thousand different forms of the Buddhist teachings, the different schools and different systems are merely different faces of the one reality. That reality is the flow of action that arises from the teachings.

In our discussions, Brother Man would say, "I don't understand why intellectuals don't study such a deep tradition as Buddhism. The Buddhism that is followed by the majority of people doesn't fully reflect what Buddhism is about, but instead gets mixed with superstitions. What can we do, Brother, to bring Buddhism back to the intellectuals?

"You know that during the Ly and Tran dynasties of Vietnam, Buddhism was practiced by the people and the majority of intellectuals embraced Buddhism. Buddhism contributed a great deal to that era. But later on Buddhism became mixed with different cultural elements, such as superstition, and was misunderstood.

"I see how monasteries can radiate actively the spirit of Buddhism, but very few people come into contact with them to see this."

"Exactly, in Hue there are the Buddhist institutes of Tay Thien and Bao Quoc, in South Vietnam there is Luong Xuyen Association of Buddhist Studies, and in North Vietmam there is the Northern Buddhist Association. There are good-hearted people who are sincerely trying to bring Buddhism back into everyday life. It is also up to monks like us to carry this responsibility. When we graduate from Bao Quoc Institute we will make efforts to bring Buddhism to the young people. We will set up Buddhist schools and hospitals like in the Ly and Tran eras.

"I see how long the road is, but I am really inspired by the ideal to reform Buddhism."

I quietly absorbed what he had said, then said slowly, "The task of reforming Buddhism demands a revolution in the teachings and the regulations of the Buddhist institutes. When the training can form a sufficient number of good students, then there can be a real reform of Buddhism. We have no choice but to bring Buddhism back into everyday life. War has waged disaster. Separation and hatred has reached a high degree. There are so many agonizing cries of death, hunger, and imprisonment. How can anyone feel peace of mind by dwelling undisturbed in a monastery?"

Every time we discussed the future we felt moved to the depths of our souls. The path was beautiful but full of thorns. Our only resources were our hopes, goodwill, our books on monastic discipline and fine manners, the *Encouraging Words of Master Quy Son* and the years studying at Bao Quoc Buddhist Institute. Will we really be able to do something?

THE NEW YEAR BELL

W e assumed that we were the first to come back home after the evacuation, but it was not so. When we had arrived at the land surrounding the Spring of Yang Hill, we found that there were already several families who had come back almost half a month earlier. On the path up the mountain that led back to the temple, the grass had grown so high that it almost hid the path. There were only six of us and there was not one of us who did not want to return as quickly as possible to the temple. We had been away for several months — how could we not be longing to return? Brother Man was in front leading the group. He seemed to be the most impatient of us all. Even the elder brothers who were usually calm and silent couldn't help expressing their eagerness.

Our journey back to the temple was slow, and like explorers we had to push aside the overgrowth in order to make a path. We were not wearing our long robes; they were rolled up in our supply sacks that we carried over our shoulders or in our hands. We had been walking for five or six days! We felt as though we were falling apart — our bodies ached and we suffered from weariness. Yet, as we approached the temple, our fatigue dissipated. Although we sensed a heavy air of silence and fear as we passed through the small hamlets that sprawled along the hills and mountains, there were signs of life and that lightened our spirits.

"There's the temple!" Brother Man suddenly cried out in joy. Under the shade of the tall pine trees appeared the temple roof, like the sudden appearance of an old friend from the distant past. The sight was very moving for all of us. I was anxious about Auntie Tu. Was she alive and safe? When we were given orders to evacuate, Auntie Tu decided to stay and take care of the temple. There was nothing we could say to dissuade her.

"Please, Brothers, you go," she had said. "You must stay alive so that you can be of use to the Dharma. I will stay here to take care of the temple. Don't try to change my mind. I'm already too old, and if anything should happen to me, there is nothing for me to regret."

We tried using authority, but in the end we had to let her

stay. I carefully pointed out to her places where she could hide when she heard gunfire, and showed her how to conceal rice and other food supplies. Only after all that could be done was done, and after praying to the Buddhas for Auntie's safety, did I join the other monks on our journey.

My worries about her safety disappeared as soon as we stepped onto the temple grounds. From afar I saw the figure of Auntie in her long, faded brown robe drawing water from the fountain. Brother Man called to her. Auntie put down the pail and looked up. When she saw us, she ran towards us. Overcome with emotion, Auntie could not speak, she just cried.

The temple roof was pelted with bullets and was damaged in many places. The temple walls were also pierced here and there with bullets. But aside from the bullet holes, the temple was not as bad off as other places. Our biggest joy, and that of Aunt Tu's, was that all of us who evacuated returned safely.

It was the 27th of the last month of the lunar calendar when we returned to the temple. That evening, the meal prepared by Auntie Tu was the first decent meal we had eaten in a long time. During the months we spent in the mountains, we had not eaten regularly; food was scarce, and not one of our meals could be called a real meal. The soy sauce we took with us we diluted with salty water. We stretched the meager rice supply by mixing in potatoes — each bowl had one-third rice and two-thirds potatoes — and even that was strictly rationed. Every one of us lost weight. On top of that, we had no beds or straw mattresses to lie on and we were overexposed to the sun. After a good dinner that night, we all went to bed and slept like logs until the morning.

The next day we began the work of cleaning up. Everything in the temple was cleaned and put back to the way it had been before. We were determined to have a celebration for the lunar New Year, the Year of the Mouse.

That whole day we were as happy as if we had seen a messenger of peace. But when night came, the ambience of war and death returned. The sound of guns could be heard in all directions. Bullets flew over our roof. We stayed in our rooms, the doors tightly bolted. Now and then the light of a flare bomb shot into the sky was visible through gaps in the walls. It would be followed by a succession of machine-gun fire.

I sat in the Ancestor Hall with Brother Man, beside an oil lamp that was burning very low. We thought about the scenes of death elsewhere and each of us quietly prayed to the Buddha for those who were unfortunate. Time passed and the night became still, yet it was an oppressive silence.

Since the day of our return, Brother Man had not invited the Great Bell. Auntie Tu would not allow it. She told us that one night she had mounted the stairs to the bell landing and had invited five to six sounds of the bell when she heard a noise coming from below. She immediately ran down and saw five or six foreign soldiers. They threatened her with their guns and warned her never to invite the bell again. Perhaps they feared the bells were a code for the enemy, or they did not want to hear the sound of the Great Bell. Every evening and every morning from then on, Auntie did not dare to invite any sounds.

"Without the bells," Auntie said softly, "the mornings and evenings seem so empty."

It was true. There was nothing more empty and cold than not hearing the sounds of the Great Bell. The atmosphere in the temple became dismal. The mountains and forest felt more remote and wild. The crickets sounded hoarser and gloomier. We usually got up at four in the morning in the temple. After having washed our faces and hands, we used to sit on our beds listening to the sounds of the Great Bell and practicing mindful breathing, or evoking the Buddha's name. Now in the early morning there were no longer any sounds of the bell. We felt something of great significance was missing. I couldn't continue with sitting meditation. For the past two to three days we had found warmth and comfort by sitting together; it helped us forget that there were no sounds of the Great

Bell. The chanting sessions also lacked something and seemed duller. The sound of the small bell in the hall seemed too weak — it did not have the strength to chase away the dismal atmosphere of the hills and mountains during the dark nights and the heavy misty dawns.

Of course we did not want the New Year to arrive in such a dreary and morose atmosphere. Obeying instructions from the older monks, we brought out the incense and candleholders and other ceremonial things for the altar and polished them until they were shiny. Aunt Tu had already started preparing the special New Year's dishes. She soaked rice and mung beans to make rice cakes. During our free time, we helped her cut banana leaves. "I'll definitely be able to make a pot of earth cakes for us." And so she set her hands to work, and we happily helped her.

Then, on the 29th, Brother Man had a wonderful idea. "We can make some sweets to celebrate the New Year." When I asked what we would make them from, he said, "We can simply make them from sweet potatoes and manioc roots." We set to work right away gathering potatoes and manioc roots from the temple garden.

Auntie Tu had cleverly cut the stems of the manioc roots to ground level a fortnight ago, to prevent thieves from digging up the roots as they did the potatoes. At a distance, the manioc patch looked as though it had just been planted a month earlier with its new sprouts and no one suspected that the roots underground were big enough to eat.

We asked Auntie Tu to buy black sugar from the small store that was temporarily opened at the bottom of Spring of Yang Hill. She bought some ginger, too. In the end, our candy was just a mixture of sweet potatoes with a little toasted ginger. That was all! Yet, it was a rare treat for the New Year during such impoverished times.

It was very reassuring to know that we still had enough rice left until next year's harvest. Before the evacuation, six or seven monks had worked hard to bury rice in very large containers in the backyard. We had faith that the following year's crop would provide enough for our needs.

On New Year's Eve, all of us — teachers, brothers, and Aunt Tu — sat in the center of the house around the fire where the rice cakes boiled in a pot. Outside, the night was chilly and pitch black. A few stars shone dimly in the sky. There was scattered gunfire. We talked, waiting for midnight when we could bring in the New Year and bow to Maitreya Buddha's spirit.

That New Year's Eve, there were only seven of us at the temple. Our venerable teacher had gone straight from our mountain refuge with four other teachers to visit an old devastated temple, and had not yet returned. Sitting by the fire, I thought a lot about our master, our respected elder. On the day of the evacuation, he had encouraged us to leave while he himself wanted to stay behind. None of us wanted to go, but because there was an order to evacuate the whole village, we couldn't refuse. We pleaded with our venerable master not to stay behind by himself. If he had insisted on staying, we would have stayed, too — which would have been defying the government's order — but reluctantly, our venerable master agreed, and we all left together. He said, "If we have sown the seeds of disaster, no matter where we go, we will not be able to avoid the consequences."

I will always remember those words and it is only now that I begin to see the truth it conveys. There were countless poor families who remained safe although they stayed behind. Yet, there were countless richer families who met with ruin and injury although they tried to find safety. By trying to avoid danger, these people met danger. As Auntie Tu put it, "In this time there is danger in all directions. It is only our merits that count; you cannot rely on wealth or intelligence." Perhaps the safest outfit to wear is made from loving kindness and compassion, and to live accordingly. Merit or fortune is created by the individual; it does not come about by accident or chance.

Auntie Tu took big rolls of earth cakes from the pot; they

were steaming hot. Midnight and the New Year were nearing. We prepared ourselves for the ceremony. The fragrance of the incense filled the Buddha Hall. I went to stand in the bell tower looking out in all directions. The mountains and forests were in darkness. The few stars in the sky flittered as if ready to fall. Looking out into the night, not a single lamp could be seen. Surely the villagers, locked behind their bolted doors, were awake and paying respect to the ancestors as they prepared to welcome in the New Year.

Brother Tam Man quietly drew near. "It is not acceptable that the sounds of the Great Bell and the drum playing the Prajñaparamita music will not accompany the New Year ceremony."

It was as if a shock went through me, as though I were just awakened from a dream. It was true, how can there be no *prajña* bell and drum to bring in the New Year? Every year for the New Year ceremony, the temple always invited the bell and drum for seven rounds. And it was these sounds that always marked the time to light the fireworks to celebrate the New Year. They would light up the sky and echo throughout the hamlets and village lying at the foot of the hills and mountains. This year no one would dare light fireworks, but that shouldn't mean that the bell and drum had to be silent, too. We turned our gaze outward. The mountains and hills, the hamlets and village were all buried in thick darkness. How could the New Year arrive in such a heavy atmosphere of fear?

"Why don't we just invite the bell and drums as usual?" I asked.

Brother Man looked startled. "And what if the French soldiers started firing guns, then what?"

I considered this. But with the thought of an entire year about to begin so full of dreariness, my courage returned. "Don't worry, they also know that today is New Year's Eve. Let's just do it. This atmosphere is too heavy; how can the New Year even dare to enter? Let's just go ahead and invite the bell and drum, Brother, and if they come, I know French, I'll explain." Seeing my determination, Brother Tam Man became more confident, and he went to the tower and began to beat the drum.

Boong…. Boong. Softly, gently, the sound of the Great Bell chimed in and began to get louder and louder, following the rhythm of the drum. There followed powerful thundering drumbeats announcing the wonderful resonating sounds of the bell. The seven rounds shook the dark night in celebration of the arrival of a new year. Along with the sound of the bell, the harmonious chanting of the monks and constant beat of the wood drum in the Buddha Hall could be heard.

Brother Man put his hand on my shoulder and pointed out

into the night. "Look, Brother!" In all directions, lights flickered on in the night as the villagers welcomed the arrival of the new year. Every door seemed to be open wide. The hills and mountains lost the feeling of wildness and appeared more gentle. The magnificence and warmth of the sounds of the Great Bell had chased away the shadows of fear and dissipated the darkness. Everyone in the area felt that spring had returned to a troubled land.

The Great Bell continued to resonate; its powerful sounds vibrated with warmth and encouragement. The two of us went inside and knelt before the altar, and together with the Sangha we wholeheartedly offered a prayer for a year of peace and joy for our people and our homeland.

My Master's Robe

There are certain things that never become old and ugly. I have a worn-out and faded brown robe that I cherish above all my other robes. Although my friends jokingly called it "the robe of thirty-seven lifetimes of asceticism," I didn't see it as old or ugly at all. I wore that robe with great satisfaction during all my years of Buddhist study at Bao Quoc Temple. My teacher gave it to me when I was preparing to make the vow to live a life of awakening. Now it's so worn-out that I can't actually wear it anymore, but it remains a precious memory of my years as a novice monk.

At the time that I asked permission to enter the temple as a novice, an aspirant to monkhood, there were almost thirty people in the community. Most of them had been in the practice for many years. There were just three of us aspirants.

Brother Tam Man joined the community one year after I did, and we became four. We all studied and worked together. Our work was harder since we had been in the practice for the shortest time. In our first year we studied the daily liturgy and precepts of novices. In our second year we studied the commentaries on the precepts and well-known sutras. By the third year, of the four of us, Brother Man and I had excelled in our studies and we had great hopes of being the first to have novice ordination. Novice ordination meant to officially take the vows of a monk. We awaited this moment as though we were waiting for some great success. For me, I yearned for this moment even more than a scholar might yearn for the announcement of the results of an exam taken after many years of study.

That moment finally came. One evening as I was carrying wood back to the temple, I was given the good news by Brother Tam Man. My teacher, the elder of the community, would officially transmit to me novice ordination and I would be sent to the Institute of Buddhist Studies of Bao Quoc. It would be just me — I was the only one of the right age and capable to begin the studies. Brother Tam Man, although capable, was two years younger than me and still not officially old enough for ordination.

In my joy, there was all the elation of youth. Suddenly I felt more mature and important. Brother Tam Man sincerely shared in my joy. The opening of the academic year at the Institute of Buddhist Studies was fast approaching. Brother Man and I discussed everything I would need to do. As for the ordination ceremony, the older monks would take care of that. I had only to review the four books of the novice Vinaya. We decided that I should send a letter home to ask for a small amount of money so that Auntie Tu could buy some incense, flowers, and fruits in Ben Ngu to offer to the Buddha on the day of my ordination. Along with sticky rice and beans, we asked Auntie Tu to cook sweet rice dessert to offer to the Sangha on this most memorable day of any monastic's life. It was uncertain, however, if the letter would arrive on time because my home was far away. We expressed our concern to Auntie Tu and she smiled in her sweet way. "Young brothers, just send the letter and if the money does not arrive on time, I will use the kitchen allowance to buy these things for you. You can repay it later on."

Happy that Auntie Tu was taking care of this, we began to prepare my trunk. Brother Man brought a pile of gold and silver paper to put in my trunk. These gold and silver pieces of paper were offered to the temple by people who came from far and wide. My teacher told us not to burn these pieces of paper but to use them to copy the sutras on. Over the past few years we had been practicing our writing by copying the sutras on these sheets of papers. Afraid I would not have enough paper to write on, Brother Tam Man brought a pile to fill a whole corner of my trunk.

My ordination was scheduled for four o'clock the next morning. That night after the Sangha's Pure Land chanting practice, I saw my teacher sitting in his room on a cushion beside the light of a flickering candle; there was a stack of old scriptures piled high on a table next to him. He was carefully mending a tear in an old brown robe. Despite his old age, he still had clear vision and a straight posture. Brother Man and I stopped at the entrance and watched. As he slowly pulled the needle through the cloth, my teacher looked like a bodhisattva in deep meditation.

After a moment we entered the room and my teacher looked up. Seeing us, he nodded and then lowered his head to continue sewing a half-sewn stitch. Brother Tam Man spoke: "Respected teacher, please go and rest, it is already very late."

My teacher did not look up. "Let me finish sewing this robe so that Quan can wear it tomorrow morning."

Then I understood why my teacher had been sorting through his pile of old robes all afternoon; he was looking for the least worn robe to fix and make presentable for me. Tomorrow for the first time I would wear a brown robe. During the past three years we were only allowed to wear the gray

robe. Once ordained as a novice, I would be allowed to put on the precious robe that the sutras call the robe of liberation, the uniform of freedom.

In a wavering voice I said, "Respected teacher, let us ask Auntie Tu to finish the sewing."

"No, I want to sew it for you with my own hands," he replied, softly.

There was silence.

With our arms folded in an obedient manner we stood to one side not daring to say another word. A little later my teacher, without raising his eyes from the needle, spoke,

"Have you heard the story in the sutra about a great disciple during the time of the Buddha who attained enlightenment just from sewing robes?

"Let me tell it to you," he continued. "This disciple often found joy and peace in mending torn robes; he mended his own and also those of his Dharma brothers. Each time he passed the needle through the fabric, he gave rise to a wholesome goodness that had the power to liberate. One day, when the needle was passing through the fabric, he understood thoroughly a deep and most wonderful teaching, and in six consecutive stitches he attained the six miraculous powers."

I turned my head and looked at my teacher with deep affection and respect. My teacher might not have attained the six miraculous powers, but he had reached a profound stage that who knew how long it would take us to achieve.

At last the robe was mended. My teacher signaled for me to come closer. He asked me to try it on. The robe was a little too large for me, but that did not stop me from feeling so happy that I was moved to tears. I was touched. Living the path of practice, I received the most sacred kind of love — a pure love that was gentle and spacious, which nourished and made fragrant my aspiration throughout my many years of training and practice.

My teacher handed me the robe. I received it knowing it was tremendous encouragement and given with a tender and discreet love. My teacher's voice at that moment was probably the gentlest and sweetest I had ever heard:

"I mended this myself so that tomorrow you will have it to wear, my child."

It was so simple. But I was deeply moved when I heard these words. Although my body at the time was not kneeling before the Buddha, and my mouth was not uttering the great vow to save all beings, my heart made the vast and deep vow with all sincerity to live a life of service. Brother Tam Man looked at me with wholehearted affection and respect. In that moment the universe for us was truly a universe of fragrant flowers.

Since that day, I have had many new robes. The new brown robes are given attention for some time but later on they are forgotten. But the old torn brown robe from my past will always remain holy. Whenever I wore this robe in the past I remembered my teacher. Today, the robe is too torn to be worn, but I still hold onto it so that in moments of reflection I can look back on the beautiful memories of the past.

HUMANITY

"You have a letter, Brother. I put it on your table."

"Where's the letter from, Brother Man?"

"Probably from France. I didn't look closely, I only remember it had an unusual stamp."

Thinking it was a letter from Thanh Luong, I was overjoyed. But no, it turned out to be a reply for a subscription to the magazine *La Pensée Bouddhique.* For over two years I had not heard any news from Thanh Luong and I didn't know where to write him. But I never stopped thinking about him, this young foreign friend whom I loved dearly. Yes, he is a young Frenchman. Thanh Luong was the name I had given him. His real name is Marty, Daniel Marty.

Thanh Luong and I were brought together by fate near my beloved temple Bao Quoc in 1947. After my teacher sent me to study at the Buddhist Institute of Bao Quoc, I would return once a month to visit my root temple. Although I only needed to go through Nam Giao and cross two small hills lined with pine tree to return to the temple, the road was very treacherous. The French army occupied all of Nam Giao region and had set up a military base there. Occasionally monks or novices took the remote paths in this region, but hardly anyone else dared pass through the area, especially the city dwellers of Hue, who had just returned after being evacuated. Even though Bao Quoc Temple was situated near a train station, hardly anyone risked coming there, which speaks for itself.

People living high in the hills had set up small fortresses for protection. There were times when gunshots were exchanged between French and Vietnamese soldiers. There were nights when the villagers shut themselves in their homes, bracing against the barrage of gunfire. And in the morning when they awoke, they found corpses near Nam Giao from the battle of the previous night, with slogans written in whitewash mixed with blood on the road. It was during these tumultuous times that Than Luong and I met. I was a Vietnamese student monk and he was a young French army soldier.

One morning after precept recitation, a time when the entire Sangha gathers to review their practice of the precepts for the previous two weeks, I set out for my temple. It was quite early; the dew was still on the tips of the grass. Inside my cloth bag I carried my sanghati robe and a few sutras. In my hand I held a cone-shaped straw hat. I felt light, and joyful at the thought of visiting my temple and seeing my teacher and Brother Tam Man, and the ancient, venerated temple.

I had just crossed a hill when a voice called out. On the hill above the road, I saw a French soldier waving. Thinking he was making fun of me because I was a monk, I turned my back to him and continued down the road. But suddenly I had the feeling that this was no joking matter. Behind me came I heard the clomping of soldier's boots as someone ran towards me. Perhaps he wanted to search me; the cloth bag I was carrying may have looked suspicious to him. I stopped walking and waited. A young soldier with a handsome and intelligent face approached me.

"Where are you going?" he asked. Hearing his poor pronunciation of *"di dau,"* I surmised that he probably knew only a few words in Vietnamese.

I laughed and asked him in French, "If I reply in Vietnamese, would you understand?"

Seeing that I could speak French, his face beamed. He let me know that he had no intention of searching me, and that he only wanted to ask me something. I asked what that was, and he replied, "I want to know which temple you're from."

"I'm from Bao Quoc Temple," I replied.

"Bao Quoc Temple? Is that the big temple on the hill near the train station?"

"That's the one," I said.

He pointed up to a water pump house on the side of the hill and said, "If you're not too busy, please come up there with me so we can talk for a little while." We sat down near the pump house and he told me about the visit he and five other soldiers had made ten days earlier to Bao Quoc Temple. They went to the temple at ten o'clock at night in search of Vietnamese resistors who were reportedly gathering at the temple.

"We were determined to find them. We carried guns. The orders were to arrest and even kill if necessary. But when we entered the temple we were utterly shocked."

"Because there were so many Viet Minh?"

"No! No!" he exclaimed, "We wouldn't have been shocked if we had seen Viet Minh. We would have attacked no matter how many there were."

It sounded very strange. "So what shocked you?"

"What happened this time was so unexpected. Wherever we did searches in the past, people would run away or be thrown into a state of panic."

"It's because the people have been terrorized so many times

that they run away in fear," I said.

"I myself don't make a habit of terrorizing or threatening people," he replied. "Perhaps it was because they have been harmed by those who came before us that they are so frightened.

"When we entered the temple," he continued, "it was like entering a deserted place. The oil lamps were turned very low. It was completely silent. We purposely stomped our feet loudly on the gravel, but there was no other sound. I had the feeling there were many people in the temple, but it was completely quiet apart from the ticking of a clock that was hanging nearby. The shouting of a comrade made me uneasy. No one made a reply. I pointed my flashlight into the empty room, and before our eyes appeared a solemn scene of fifty or sixty monks sitting still and silently in meditation."

"It was because you came during our sitting period," I said, nodding my head.

"Yes, it was like we ran into a strange and invisible force," he said. "It scared us so much that we turned and left the temple. The monks just ignored us! They didn't raise a voice in reply and they didn't show any signs of panic or fear."

"They weren't ignoring you, they were practicing concentrating on their breath, that was all."

"We ourselves were attracted to their calmness — it was

worthy of our respect. We stood silently in the temple's court-yard at the foot of a large tree and waited for perhaps a half an hour. There were a series of bells that sounded, and then the temple returned to normal activity. A monk lit a torch and came to invite us inside, but we simply told him why we were there and then asked to leave. From that day on I began to change my ideas about the Vietnamese people.

"There are many young men about our age among us," he began. "We are homesick; we miss our families and country a lot. We have been sent here to kill the Viet Minh, but we don't know if we will kill them or we will be killed by them and never return home to our families. Seeing the people here work so hard to rebuild their shattered lives reminds me of the shattered lives of my relatives in France. The peaceful and serene life of those Vietnamese monks makes me think about the lives of all human beings on this Earth. And I wonder why we have come here. What is this hatred between the Viet Minh and us that we have come all this way to fight them?"

Deeply moved, I took the hand of the young soldier. I told him a story of an old friend of mine who had enlisted to fight the French, and who had been successful in winning many battles. One day my friend came to the temple and burst into tears as he embraced me. He told me that during an attack on a fortress, while he was concealed behind some rocks, he saw two young French soldiers sitting and talking. "When I saw the bright, handsome, and innocent faces of those young boys," he said, "I couldn't bear to open fire, dear Brother. People can label me weak and soft, they can say that if all the Vietnamese fighters were like me, it wouldn't be long before our whole country was overtaken. But, oh mother, for a moment I had loved the enemy like my own mother loves me! I knew that the deaths of these two youngsters would make their mothers in France suffer, just as my mother had grieved for the death of my younger brother."

"So you see," I said, "the young Vietnamese soldier's heart was filled with the love of humanity."

The young French soldier was lost in thought for a moment. Perhaps like me, he had realized the absurdity of the killing, the calamity of war, and that young men were dying in an unjust and heartbreaking way.

The sun had already risen high in the sky and it was time to go. Before going he told me that his name was Daniel Marty and he was twenty-one years old. He had just finished high school before he came to Vietnam. He showed me photographs of his mother and a younger brother and sister. We parted with a feeling of understanding between us and he promised to visit me at the temple on Sundays.

From then on our friendship continued to deepen. I spoke

to him about Buddhism and he let me borrow books on Buddhism written by Rhys David, Neel, La Vallee Poussin. He had an affinity towards Buddhism and wanted to live the way of a Buddhist. I took him to the Buddha Hall for prostration practice and I gave him the Dharma name Thanh Luong. He was very happy when I explained the meaning of the name, "Pure and Refreshing Peaceful Life." I taught him Vietnamese and after a few months he was able to converse a little with Brother Tam Man.

We became close to him. He told me that he no longer had to go on raids as he had previously done. If there were letters from home he showed them to me. Whenever he saw me he joined his palms in greeting just like any Buddhist.

One day, Brother Man suggested that we invite our friend to a vegetarian meal at the temple. Thanh Luong accepted the invitation happily. Our Dharma friend highly praised the delicious black olives and the flavorful dishes we served him. He found the fragrant mushroom rice soup Brother Man had prepared so delicious that he couldn't believe it was vegetarian. I had to explain to him in detail how it was made before he would believe that it was true.

There were days when, sitting beside the temple tower, we would delve into conversations on spirituality and literature. When I praised French literature, Thanh Luong's eyes lit up with pride of his nation's culture. I outlined a short history of Vietnamese literature for him from its foundation in ancient times. Our friendship was becoming very deep. Then one day when he came to visit, he announced that his unit would be moving to another area and it was likely that he would be able to return to France. Our farewell was sad and compassionate.

"I'll never forget your gentle face, Brother," he said. "Buddhism has made your spirit calm and gentle, pure and compassionate. I don't know if I will ever be able to see you again."

I walked him to the gate under the arch of the three portals of Bao Quoc Temple and looked him in the eye as I spoke. "No matter where you are, if you keep the Dharma in mind then I will always be beside you. The Dharma has brought us together to understand and like one another. I am certain your heart will always be bright and wholesome because there is a Buddha in you. As children of the Buddha, we will never be parted."

"I will write you, Brother."

"And I will be very happy to receive your letter."

A month later I received a letter from him with news that he would return to France, then go to Algeria. He promised to write to me from there.

I have not heard from him since then. Who knows where Thanh Luong, that child of the Buddha, is now. Is he safe? But I have faith that no matter what situation he is in, he is at peace. The lives of all living beings filled his own heart, and like my Vietnamese friend, he too saw the meaninglessness and destructiveness of war.

So many young, handsome men have been thrown into the throes of death! So many innocent lives — not yet having had the chance to taste the goodness of life — have been thrown into a blazing fire of death, like so many mayflies. And for what? Does anyone know? When will the bloodshed end? Will there ever be an end to mothers anxiously waiting for their children to return home? This I ask of my young Vietnamese friends and the young people of France, and, indeed, young people all over the world! You have not yet experienced life — you are still innocent! You should not be forced into the meaningless bloodshed of war!

The sound of the bell rang out in the evening as the sun was setting.

Daniel! Thanh Luong! Somewhere across the oceans can you hear the echoes of the temple bell? Pray for the stream of compassionate nectar of the Buddhas to quickly put out the flames of human violence!

Parallax Press publishes books and tapes on mindful awareness and social responsibility. We carry all books and tapes by Thich Nhat Hanh. For a copy of our free catalog, please write to:

Parallax Press
P.O. Box 7355
Berkeley, California 94707
www.parallax.org

Thich Nhat Hanh has retreat communities in southwestern France (Plum Village), Vermont (Green Mountain Dharma Center), and California (Deer Park Monastery), where monks, nuns, laymen, and laywomen practice the art of mindful living. For information about retreats or local Sanghas practicing in the tradition of Thich Nhat Hanh, visit www.iamhome.org or write to:

Plum Village
13 Martineau
33580 Dieulivol, France
www.plumvillage.org

Green Mountain Dharma Center
P.O. Box 182
Hartland Four Corners, VT 05049

Deer Park Monastery
2499 Melru Lane
Escondido, CA 92026